Elsabé Brink

1899:
THE LONG MARCH
HOME

A little-known incident in the
Anglo-Boer War

Kwela Books

Cover design Karen Ahlschläger
Typography by Nazli Jacobs
Set in 11 on 14pt Photina
Printed and bound by National Book Printers,
Drukkery Street, Goodwood, Western Cape

First edition, first printing 1999

ISBN 0-7957-0089-X

CONTENTS

As a young man, Peka ka Dinizulu, a lifelong friend of J S Marwick, accompanied him on the march. He recited the *izibongo* – praise poem – at Marwick's funeral. *(Courtesy Clare Rossouw)*

J S Marwick as a young man of 25. This photograph was taken a
few days after he completed the long march from Johannesburg to
Natal. *(Courtesy Clare Rossouw)*

Father! Muhle! whose daring trails are without equal.
Uprooter of objectionable barriers and obstructions,
To the satisfaction of all peoples.
Conqueror of drifts in defiance even of Paul Kruger,
Forcing them to give way, even Piet Joubert.

Those of olden times acclaimed that fighting bulls were drawn from yearlings.
Constantly present were the broad-brimmed hats of Piet Joubert.
He heard not by repute, and required no telling, but saw for himself.
Collected the waifs and strays, and so rejoiced even those who knew him not.

He assailed and both the North and the South resounded with his deeds.
Also came those of the West to announce to those of the East.
Within his precincts crowds were ever present,
Extolling the man they called Muhle.

And appeared the spoilers prying even into rubbish heaps.
Oh! How envy springs from the eye to affect the heart!
Following the trails of a buffalo without seeking advice from those ahead,
To expend their useless efforts amongst hovels and temporary shelters.

Long may you live, MUHLE!
And may the Great Spirit preserve you.
There was never a courtier without blemish.
Helper of the needy and orphans,
Even the penniless will hail you as a hero.
Only the dead are appreciated, not the living.

In 1915 Alfred Kumalo wrote an *izibongo* – praise poem – on Marwick and his confrontation with
Paul Kruger and Piet Joubert. It was sent to Marwick in 1941. This English translation is by
H C Lugg. *(Courtesy Clare Rossouw)*

"Izibongo zika Muhle."

Gwagwa lakwa Zulu
elipungela usapo lwakwa Mnyamana.
Gwagisa ka Ndaba no Punga
owa didiyela o Mtshikila ba gewaneka.
Silo esomuntu esibuk' emehlweni,
Ku kohlwe no Kumbulayo
Sindiyandiya esa dida ibandhla,
o Stofela nama gqweta akwake.
Umazunge i izintala ku xwaye igulu.
Luti oluhlokoza izinyosi zilikizela.
Akani elizela umkondo wamabunu,
abati bayambamba, wa gwinja
Ukahlamba walungamula pakati
no dwendwe lwake.
Mamba eluhlaza eyaba nguma ngomsila
Lokoza kwaba lokotayo.
Silawuli sebandhla kwahleka no Dumba
'Mbuzi ka Damenza abayibamba nge
ndhlebe yabekezela."
Kawuzela ufo ka Marwick
ulu pambili.
Umenjalo wena ka Ndaba.
Ho kanjana ludhliwa nje siya kumbulana.
(apelile, angi mbongi yaluto).

This *izibongo* – also on Marwick, known as Muhle, praises his bravery and personality. Marwick is likened to a snake, the mamba which kills its enemies with a mere flick of its tail, leaving others dumbfounded by this feat. The poem is written in classical Zulu. *(Courtesy Clare Rossouw)*

PREFACE

October 1899: Johannesburg, heart of the Witwatersrand, teetered on the brink of war. 'From being a busy, flourishing hive of energetic workers of all descriptions crowded to excess, fearing accidents at every street corner, seething with life, hope and ambition, aided by ferment of political unrest, Johannesburg became a deserted, gloomy, empty city with what appeared to our overstrung nervous minds to be a rapacious bloodthirsty horde at its gates ...'[1] This was how an English woman, Isabella Lipp, captured the mood of the city.

It had taken fourteen short years – from 1886 to 1899 – for the Witwatersrand to become the richest gold-field in the world. The gold-ore was not of a very high quality, but there were vast reserves of gold along a reef which stretched for almost 50 kilometres along the surface and to a depth of more than 600 metres. In 1895, the Witwatersrand, also called the Rand or the Reef, yielded gold valued at £8.5 million, about 20 per cent of all the gold produced annually in the world. In 1898, despite problems and recurrent recessions, the Witwatersrand gold mines were producing gold worth £15 million and were expecting to produce gold worth more than £20 million in 1899.

Profits, in the form of dividends, were equally promising. From 1897 to 1898 Witwatersrand gold dividends had risen from £2.5 million to £4.8 million. Gold reserves were estimated to be worth some £700 million. And mine-owners believed that a clear profit of at least some £200 million could be made. The question was, who would control these riches?

This treasure trove lay in the territory of the Zuid-Afrikaansche Republiek (ZAR), one of four white territories at the southern tip of Africa. Compared to the Orange Free State and the two British colonies, the Cape and Natal, the ZAR was the poorest, the most backward and administratively the least competent. It was in the windswept, treeless grassland of the ZAR highveld, far from highways or rivers, that a new city called Johannesburg sprung up. Johannesburg was unlike any other city or town in the world. This tent and tin town was rough, bustling, noisy, cosmopolitan and dangerous – and many referred to it as the new Sodom and Gomorrah.

Before the arrival of the railways in 1893, Johannesburg could be reached only on horseback, by stagecoach, ox-wagon or on foot. Nevertheless, the gold strike had attracted people from all over the globe: from Alaska, California, Russia, Canada, Great Britain and the far-flung corners of the British Empire such as Australia, New Zealand and India, as well as territories in the rest of southern Africa. The population on the Rand increased rapidly. Between 1892 and 1895 the number of African minework-ers on the Rand doubled from 24 000 to 50 000 and quadrupled to 97 800 in 1899. Local white ZAR burghers and their families also flocked to Johannes-burg in search of a better life, but were soon vastly outnumbered by foreigners. By 1895 there were at least seven white male Uitlanders, as the foreigners were called, for every three white male ZAR burghers. In a society where only white men could vote, would ZAR citizens be outvoted in their own country?

Most Uitlanders were British citizens. Very few had been given the right to vote in the ZAR. To have given these vast numbers of Uitlanders the franchise, in the eyes of many burghers, was tanta-mount to giving up the Transvaal, as the ZAR was also called. The Jameson Raid had made the burghers even more deter-mined not to give the Uitlanders the right to vote. The Jameson Raid – a political blunder of some magnitude – had taken place in December 1895 when Dr Leander Starr Jameson and his 500 colonial troops invaded the ZAR on the pretext of coming to the aid of the Uitlanders. After the raid, the ZAR government tried to address the grievances of the Uitlanders,

but tensions increased significantly between the ZAR government of President Paul Kruger and the British government which maintained that it was protecting the interests of its citizens on the gold-fields.

In April 1897 Sir Alfred Milner was appointed as the new Lieutenant-Governor of the Cape Colony. He thought that the situation in South Africa could be solved in one of two ways: either President Kruger had to be forced to make substantial reforms, or there had to be war.

In January 1899 Johannesburg was a town filled with rumours and counter-rumours about the 'situation', as the growing tension between the ZAR and the British Empire was referred to. Many Uitlanders had already abandoned their jobs, businesses and homes and sought refuge in Durban and Cape Town.

In 1903 Francis Harrison recalled the events which preceded the war: 'In 1898 a vigorous agitation against the oppres-sive rule of the Kruger clique began, and resulted in a great demonstration on the shooting, in December 1898, of a [British] subject named Edgar by a Johannesburg policeman. During the year of 1899 great mass meetings were held by the Uitlanders, and finally the Boer Government broke off negotiations consequent upon the Bloemfontein Conference, and issued its ultimatum to Great Britain.'[2]

Some eighty years later Thomas Pakenham summarised the subsequent clash between the Boers and the British which became known either as the

Anglo-Boer War, or the South African War or the Second War of Independence: 'The war declared by the Boers on 11 October 1899 gave the British in Kipling's famous phrase, "no end of a lesson". The British public expected it to be over by Christmas. It proved to be the longest (two and three-quarter years), the costliest (over £200 million), the bloodiest (at least twenty-two thousand British, twenty-five thousand Boer and twelve thousand African lives) and the most humiliating war for Britain between 1815 and 1914.'[3]

All the inhabitants of Johannesburg were affected by the looming war. The ZAR burghers joined the Boer commandos. Uitlanders could join the British army or flee to the coast to wait out the war. Referring to the Uitlanders who joined the British side, Francis Harrison seemed rather surprised that 'they were fully capable of self-sacrifice, and of rising above merely material considerations'. Scores of Boer women were left in town to fend for themselves as best they could, but most of the white Uitlander women fled by train to Natal and the Cape.

Isabella Lipp, who remained behind in the ZAR, recorded the departure of the refugees: 'So away they went, poor souls, enduring great hardships on the journey to a place of refuge in British territory – packed like sardines in carriages, coal trucks, animal trucks, scarcely standing room, and when the panic was at its height, foodless, without drinks for their little crying thirsty children – no shelter from the burning South African sun, white and coloured mixed indiscrimi-nately – a journey of hours taking days, stoppages at the sidings and stations for many hours while commando trains filled with Boers passed on.'[4]

Thousands of black men and women were also trapped in Johannesburg when the mines closed and their white employers fled the imminent outbreak of war. Few employers, least of all the mine-owners, took responsibility for repatriating their workers after they had been paid off. In some cases workers were forced off mine properties and had to leave the relative safety of the compounds. Many feared that if they remained on the Witwatersrand they would starve, become involved with looters and rioters, be arrested by the police as vagrants or – at worst – be shot by Boer commandos. Even though most could pay the fare, workers were not readily given passage on the departing refugee trains.

The only other alternative was to walk home, on the eve of war. It could be done, even in a country where distances were vast, where the veld was inhabited by wild animals, where frost in winter and heat and thunderstorms in summer were regular occurrences, where towns were few and far between, and where the reception of black refugees by white townspeople was uncertain. Above all in October 1899 travelling any distance would mean crossing battle lines which were being drawn. Yet we know that some people did walk home. One such march, from Johannesburg to Natal, took place from 6 to 15 October 1899.

A young white man from Natal, J S Marwick, J S or Sid to his friends, helped

13

some 7 000 Zulu workers to avoid being trapped in Johannesburg without work and without food for the duration of the war.

Marwick organised this exodus within the space of ten days and led these 7 000 workers on a long march to Natal and Zululand, a journey of almost 400 kilometres. The march happened without major incident, without fighting or people being attacked or robbed, and – amazingly – with no serious injuries or deaths along the way.

Marwick received a telegram of thanks and congratulations from the Prime Minister of Natal and from Joseph Chamberlain, the Secretary for the Colonies in Great Britain, both in recognition of this achievement and for going beyond the call of duty.

The march hit the headlines during the first weeks of the Anglo-Boer War. But except for a few lines in history books, the march was soon forgotten. Only recently historians such as Thomas Pakenham, Charles van Onselen, Peter Warwick and Diana Cammack have referred to it in passing. On reading these brief references to this event many questions remain unanswered.

What do we know about the 7 000 workers who marched home from Johannesburg? How did these young men, who had been born most probably between 1870 and 1875 in the Zulu kingdom, grow up? Why did they migrate to the Witwatersrand? What was Marwick doing on the Rand? Who became part of the march and who was turned away? What route was taken and how were the marchers received in the platteland? What happened when the marchers met with the Boer and the British armies? How were the lives of the marchers changed when the march was over? And why was the march forgotten so soon after it had happened?

The Long March Home is an attempt to tell the story of this march and to seek answers to some of these questions.   E B

Chapter 1

A CHILDHOOD IN THE ZULU KINGDOM

1870–1890

In 1870 the Zulu nation was ruled by King Mpande. It was a strong and independent kingdom, the most powerful African state south of the Limpopo River. During Mpande's long reign of thirty-two years, his followers had prospered in this fertile region with its abundant water, ideal for raising cattle, their main source of wealth. In 1872 Mpande died peacefully of old age. He was succeeded by his son, the forty-year-old Cetshwayo.

Cetshwayo inherited a kingdom which stretched from the Thukela and the Mzinyathi Rivers to the valley of the Phongolo. During the first years of his reign the population of the Zulu kingdom grew to 300 000 people and the nation's wealth – measured in cattle – increased. In the neighbouring colony of Natal, however, British government officials watched with dismay as Cetshwayo rebuilt the Zulu army and formed young men into disciplined army regiments. What kind of threat did he pose for the future, the officials wondered? And how would his reign affect British plans to bring all the colonies and republics in this region together under the British flag?

These Zulu men in regimental dress, ready to do a war dance, give some impression of what Cetshwayo's regiments would have looked like as they marched through the Zulu kingdom. *(Courtesy Transnet Heritage Library)*

Cetshwayo was on good terms with the British, but he realised that trouble was brewing. Late in 1878 he appealed for peace: 'What have I done or said to the Great House of England, which placed my father, Panda, over the Zulu Nation, and after his death put me in power? What have I done to the Great White Chief? I hear from all parts that the soldiers are around me and the Zulu Nation asked me this day what I have said to the white people. I hear that British troops are now in Swaziland, and that they are there for the purpose of fighting the Zulu Nation, and that these troops crossed through Zulu territory ... I hear that war is intended.'[1]

Cetshwayo was correct in predicting war: on 11 January 1879 the British invaded the Zulu kingdom. At the bloody battle of Isandhlwana the Zulus defeated the invading army. The British lost 1 600 soldiers in the battle – the British army's worst defeat since the Crimean War in 1858. But the local army was supported by the might of the British Empire. At the end of 1879 Great Britain had avenged its defeat, and the Zulu kingdom was forced to surrender. It was renamed Zululand.

For ten years after the Anglo-Zulu War, Zululand and its people experienced hard times. Zulus saw their king captured, their kingdom conquered, the army broken up and their country divided into thirteen separate chiefdoms. Zulus who remained loyal to the king did not accept the appointed chiefs and civil war broke out in Zululand.

In 1887 the greater part of Zululand was placed under British rule when it became the colony of British Zululand. As the new ruler, the British government imposed a hut tax of fourteen shillings on every hut in Zululand. No one was overlooked. If a man did not have enough cash to pay the tax, he had to sell his cattle to find the money. Many a chief had to send the young men in his kraal to find work outside Zululand in order to pay this annual tax.

At first the young men went to work building the railway which linked Durban with the ZAR. But news of higher wages paid on the gold-fields of the Witwatersrand, between £3 and £4 rather than thirty shillings a month, reached Zululand. Young men were willing to sign contracts with labour agents from the mines to go to the gold-fields. Some young men of the same family left Zululand in small groups under the leadership of an older relative or 'brother' to walk to the gold-fields.

How did these young men, who were born between 1870 and 1875, grow up in the Zulu kingdom before it was conquered by the British?

The picture we have comes from studies conducted on Zulu society before the British conquest of the Zulu kingdom. Zulu society as it functioned during this time was very well ordered. In traditional Zulu culture it was believed that only with age could men or women move to positions of responsibility and authority. Respect for any person older than oneself ruled the life of every man, woman and child. Strict rules which governed how one behaved before one's elders controlled almost all aspects of daily life.

Young Zulu men in traditional dress pose in front of a hut, having a meal. The man at the back moved as the picture was being taken. At the time (around the turn of the century) one had to stand very still whilst a photograph was being taken. *(Courtesy MuseuMAfricA)*

Each child born had his or her special place in the community. The community was usually made up of an *umuzi*, a homestead or family kraal. This kraal was ruled by the patriarch or *umnumzana*, who had several wives. The first or most important wife was the *undlunkulu*. She was the chief wife to whom everybody, including the other younger wives of the patriarch, had to be obedient.

Until they were eight or nine years old, small children slept with their mothers and sisters in their mothers' huts. These children were called *izingane*. They had to listen to and obey their older brothers and sisters, who had to look after them.

When they were old enough, at about five or six, the *izingane* would be sent out to herd the goats, calves and sheep. At milking time they were allowed to follow their older brothers into the kraal where they could hold the cow while a brother or father did the milking. The children often learned what was expected of them as they grew older through play.

At the *qhumbuza* ceremony, young boys had their ears pierced as a sign of their new status as older boys. With other boys of the same age group they were placed into age sets or *izintanga*. Some years later, at puberty, boys in an age set went through a series of rituals –

17

Three young children photographed in front of their huts with a married adult man, perhaps their father or grandfather. He is wearing a head-ring or *isicoco*. The eldest child, who is in charge of the others, is carrying the baby. This picture was taken early in the twentieth century. Note the enamel bowl in the grass and the dress which the baby is wearing. *(Courtesy Transnet Heritage Library)*

The interior of a Zulu hut. The pumpkins and the clay pots at the back of the hut were used for storing grain. The cast-iron three-legged pot in the fireplace indicates that the picture was taken early in the twentieth century. *(Courtesy Transnet Heritage Library)*

ukuthomba – accompanied by feasts to mark their entry into the teenage years. The boys were then called *abafana*. Each *umfana*, or boy, was honoured by a new name, by which his age mates and younger children would have to call him.

Their new status as *abafana* meant that the boys could leave their mothers' huts and now move to their own sleeping quarters – *amalawu* – which they shared with their age mates. As bigger boys, now, they were sent out each day to herd cattle for most of the day. In addition, when they were strong enough, the boys would become their fathers' mat boys or mat carriers, *udibi*. By carrying his father's baggage when he went on long journeys or going with him when he plied his trade, the *umfana* would learn the trade of his father.

The *ukubuthwa* or enrolment into regiments was the next step on the road to manhood, when teenagers became *izinsizwa*. When they were about eighteen years old, young men enrolled with their age mates in one of the king's regiments to be taught the traditional codes and way of behaving. In peace-time these age sets were put into *amakhanda*, military kraals or towns, where they served the king by collecting firewood, building, planting, hoeing and reaping and threshing the royal crops, transporting grain, carrying messages or hunting. In war-time they would be expected to go to war as well.

These young Zulu mat carriers, only in their early teens, are preparing to leave on a journey. Note the way in which they are dressed. *(Courtesy Department of Historical and Literary Papers, University of the Witwatersrand Library)*

The young men would only become mature, adult men at about the age of forty, when the king discharged his soldiers from active duty and gave them permission to marry. Only then were men considered to have the experience, wisdom and prestige to become full, mature members of their society. In an act of *ukukhehla* each man would put on the head-ring or *isicoco*. This head-ring showed that the youth had become an adult man, ready to become a father, a teacher or a master in his craft who could take on apprentices. As *izinkehli*, the married men were expected to build the framework of their wives' huts, to build or repair the fences of their kraals, to manage their cattle herds and to clear land of trees in order to prepare new fields for crops. They were also expected to visit the king on occasion. From the ranks of these mature men the king would choose chiefs who would serve him as ministers of state or as councillors. They were called his *izinduna*.

The relationship with the king worked in two directions. The king or chief could only expect all these services if he did not abuse his people. When a chief wanted to build his power, he would treat all strangers who came to his kraal with great hospitality and generosity. If they chose to serve him, they would then be included and protected in his clan.

There was little chance for common people to improve their humble background, except by doing well in battle, by gaining royal favour or by becoming skilled craftsmen or healers. Some chose to follow well-placed individuals or people of character who had considerable influence. The poor man who served a strong man was able to bask in the reflected glory and so earn respect and admiration from his friends, as well as cattle, in reward for service.

These traditional ways were still very important when Zulus began to go to the new colonial towns to find jobs. Chiefs would often send age sets of young men into town to work for wages. Elders would then use the wages that were sent home to benefit the house to which the young men belonged, or for other community purposes. These wages went towards paying government taxes, buying tribal rights to land or buying cattle. A few of these cattle would be set aside for the young man who had earned these wages, for use as bridewealth or *ilobolo*.

In towns the young men were forbidden by their elders and their social customs to take on jobs that had a status which these youngsters had not achieved. They were allowed only to hire themselves out for jobs which they would have done at home, such as doing domestic work, looking after children in the homes of the white settlers, or other jobs where they would become apprentices and which did not pay much money or had low status.

On the Witwatersrand young Zulu *abafana* often found work in a white household to look after the young children. As mat carriers, they would have gained experience in sweeping the hut, collecting firewood, putting the pot on the fire and cooking food. It was an honour – and a sign of trustworthiness too –

for a young person to serve an elder. Older people saw it as a sign of respect to be served by someone younger.

Despite the changing social ways which accompanied the discovery of gold, the power of the chiefs continued over the younger members of the community who had migrated. Even when young men began to choose where and for whom they wanted to work, their chiefs still made sure that the working conditions of their young relatives were satisfactory. Ten years after young Zulu men had started going to the mines, their chiefs still had enough power over them to order them to return home.

In December 1896, writing of the Zulu presence on the mines at this time, the *Natal Mercury* remarked: 'The news of the treatment Natives had been subjected to by the Boers had been disseminated through the length and breadth of Natal and Zululand with the result that the various chiefs had met by appointment, held an *indaba* and arrived at the conclusions that the Rand was no place for their men. Messengers were then dispatched from Natal and Zululand to warn their kindred to return at once.'[2]

Young Zulu men, like many others from southern Africa, left their homes and began a journey to the Witwatersrand to find jobs which would help pay their community's taxes, buy more cattle to replenish the herds or buy food in times of shortages or famine. On the Witwatersrand they had to adapt to a new and often dangerous world where they had to learn new skills on the mines, or put the skills they had learnt at home to the best and most profitable use.

Chapter 2

A CHILDHOOD IN COLONIAL NATAL

1870–1890

An early inhabitant described Richmond in the 1860s and 1870s as 'set prettily upon a green slope, a tiny peaceful village of thatched cottages, rose hedges and pretty gardens, which might well have been transplanted in its entirety from a county in England. No shrill railway whistles and shunting disturbed its peaceful serenity ... A couple of general stores, a modest inn, the Post Office and Magistracy, with the tiny church, comprised its public buildings. The Church of St Mary's was the first in Natal consecrated by Natal's first prelate, Bishop Colenso, and is the oldest in the Province. Built of stone, with a tiled roof and set in a bower of old trees which were the haunt of rooks and other birds, it was the counterpart of any English village church, and its simple services, heightened in beauty by sweet girlish voices, will be remembered by many old residents of Richmond, as a weekly joy to the ample congregation which filled the small temple of worship on the hill.'[1]

On 17 June 1875 John Sidney Marwick, the third son of Thomas and Elizabeth Marwick, was born in this 'tiny, peaceful' village. Marwick's mother, Elizabeth, was the daughter of a teacher, William Mackenzie.

Mackenzie had emigrated to Natal in 1850 from a village called Lurray in Caithness, Scotland. Mackenzie – and others who were struggling to make a living in England and Scotland – had been convinced by Joseph C Byrne to start a new life in the new, fertile British colony, Natal. In addition to small farms of about twenty acres per man, each child was given five acres of land as well. Each family also received a half-acre plot in the village which was to be laid out for the settlers. About three thousand men, women and children took up this offer. Mr Mackenzie accepted another offer, that of the job of schoolmaster, in this new village.

The settlers reached Natal after a long and dangerous sea voyage. One of the Byrne settlers, Ellen McLeod, described their first days at sea: 'I was this morning like one arisen from the dead. I have had five days of sickness and have taken nothing but tea and water ... Fancy the state we are all in. We have not been undressed for the last three days, but have all been in bed together sick, with teapot, a tin pot of water and a mug, and not one of us could raise our heads.'[2]

Even though she thought that her memories had 'no high adventure value', Mackenzie's daughter, Elizabeth, as an old woman, wrote down what she could remember about their journey to Africa. In old-fashioned English she began: 'In the latter part of 1849 Mr and Mrs Mackenzie and their two children, Elizabeth and Robert, aged respectively six and two, left a snow-covered Scotland and embarked in the sailing vessel *Conquering Hero* on a voyage which lasted three months. Their

Right: Little John Sidney Marwick posed as a drummer-boy for the photographer H Kisch in Pietermaritzburg. During Victorian times the intro-duction of young boys to things military started at a very early age. *(Courtesy Clare Rossouw)*
Below: Buildings on Shepstone Street in Richmond housing a local bank, the post office and the old court house just after the turn of the centruy. *(Courtesy Richmond, Byrne and District Museum)*

arrival in Durban in brilliant sunshine was an experience never to be forgotten by the little Elizabeth, who raced about revelling in freedom after months of captivity, and rejoicing in the beauty of the green grass, white sand and blue sky. When voicing her pleasure, it was a shock to the little girl to see her mother weeping, and it was not until long afterwards that she was able to understand the anguish of homesickness and fear of the future in a strange land, which had occasioned her mother's tears.'[3]

From the harbour in Durban, the Mackenzie family was taken to Richmond by a Dutch farmer, Dirk Uys. Mr Mackenzie had expected things to be organised in much the same way as in Scotland. He thought that a house would be ready for his family to move into when they arrived in Richmond. He was, after all, the new school-teacher, a respected member of society. But nothing of the kind awaited the family in Richmond, not even a shed. Dirk Uys suggested that the Mackenzies should build a shelter by covering their four-poster bed, which had come all the way from Scotland, with a tarpaulin that he would lend them. They could camp in this tent-like structure until a more permanent shelter was built. Uys also lent the family a cow so that the children had milk to drink.

Elizabeth continued her story in the third person: 'A hartebeest house was their next dwelling place, the low walls being contracted from sods and roofed with thatch, the eaves projecting so that the sod walls might not become sodden walls in a shower of rain. Later Mr Mckenzie built with his own hands a

stone house upon land which had been allotted to his daughter. This house was occupied by the family until they removed to Maritzburg. This house was then used as a magistrate's office and Court House.'

In 1863 the young Elizabeth married Thomas Marwick, a newly arrived settler. To earn his passage to Africa, Marwick had worked as a ship's carpenter and wheelwright until he reached Durban. He left his ship and found work as a teacher of woodwork at the Wesleyan Indaleni Mission Station. This mission station had been founded by the Reverend James Allison on 600 acres of land given to him by the Natal government. Allison built a mission house, outbuildings and a chapel on the land, and established a village of sixty houses for his black converts. His wife taught tailoring to the boys and dressmaking to the young black girls on the mission station. At the industrial school Marwick taught some twenty-five boys reading, writing and arithmetic, as well as building, carpentry and agriculture.

But the school did not succeed and it was closed down. The Marwicks moved back to Richmond to the house Elizabeth's father had built in Harding Street. They continued to live there for the next fifty years. Altogether they had ten children, three of whom died as babies.

The old Elizabeth Marwick reminisced: '... thus Mrs Marwick had the rather unique experience of living as maiden, young girl, wife, mother, grandmother and great-grandmother in the same village

THE MARWICKS OF RICHMOND

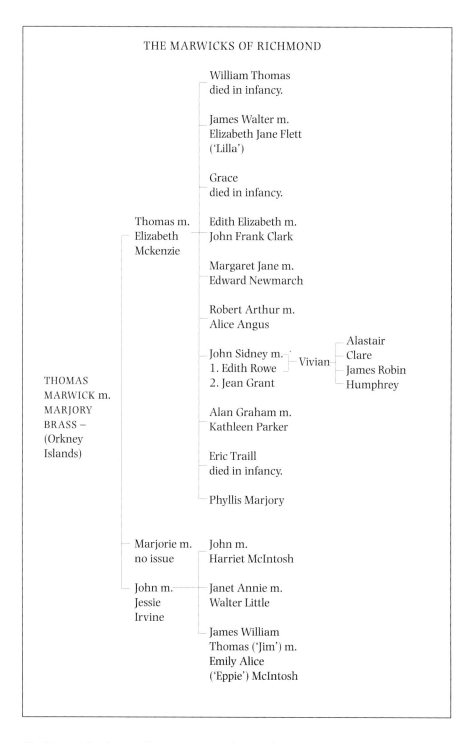

The Marwick family tree – four generations of Marwicks, circa 1850 to present. *(Adapted from Coulson (1986), Beaulieu on Illovo, p204)*

and for most of the time in the same house.'

At the house Thomas set up his own forge and wagon-building business. He became so successful that he wrote to his friend James Hackland in the Orkney Islands, as well as his mother, his brother John and his sister Marjory, suggesting that they should join him in Natal, which they did. John started a farm, *Wardhill*, close to Richmond and Marjorie soon married Peter Flett, the son of one of the other settler families.

The Marwicks became a well-known family among the British settlers who lived in the Richmond district. They served on the Richmond Agricultural Society, the Richmond Rifle Association and regularly attended services at the Richmond Wesleyan church.[4] The wooden pews and other woodwork of the church had, in fact, been made by Thomas Marwick and his pupils while he was still at Indaleni Industrial School.

After gold was discovered on the Witwatersrand, the farmers of Richmond began to send their produce to the gold-fields. They could hardly keep up with the demand and made excellent profits. In August 1889 the newspaper *Natal Mercury* commented: 'Richmond itself is a struggling village, considered by those who have seen it, the nearest approach to an English village of any in the colony. Here, the farming industry largely con-centrates, bringing its produce to the two leading merchants, Mr Henry Nicholson

The house on Harding Street, Richmond, thought to have been that of Thomas and Elizabeth Marwick. (*Courtesy Richmond, Byrne and District Museum*)

and Mr Sink – both of whom have large substantial stores and storage buildings. Mr Nicholson receives as much as 1,000 lbs. of butter per week ... It was tinned down to 2 lb. tins and sent to Johannesburg, with the handsome result of 1/- profit on every two-pound tin, in spite of Transvaal duty. This butter sold easily and had there been 50 tons, it would have gone up in smoke.'[5]

Young John Sidney Marwick, his brothers and his sisters were sent to the local school in Richmond for their education. He would most probably have started school at the age of five or six; he finished school at the age of thirteen in 1888 with an excellent school report. He finished fifth out of the 169 children who competed in the Natal colony's 'Government Certificate of Proficiency in Elementary Subjects of Instruction'. He gained 1 042 marks out of a possible total of 1 200 in the following subjects: handwriting, arithmetic, spelling from dictation, English grammar, composition (writing), geography, English history, European history, drawing and astronomy.

Marwick learnt to speak fluent Zulu as he was growing up in Natal, a skill which would have considerable importance in his future. It's likely that he learnt *isiZulu* from Zulu servants or the local Zulu children. The English and the Zulu children mixed during their free time, outside of school hours, but they did not go to school together.

'I don't know how my granddad's household was organised,' Marwick's granddaughter, Clare Rossouw, remi-

nisced. 'But when each of my brothers was born, granddad sent a young Zulu *umfana* to our home. He would be the companion of my brothers, so that they always had a young Zulu boy to play with. My brothers all speak fluent Zulu. My brother, James Robin, speaks Zulu as beautifully as my grandfather did.'

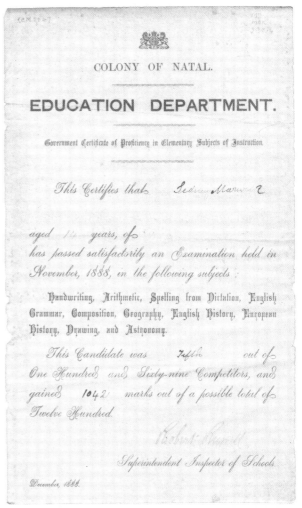

A copy of John Sidney Marwick's school-leaving certificate, December 1888. Marwick did exceptionally well – he came fifth out of the 169 scholars in the colony who took the examination. *(Courtesy Killie Campbell Africana Library)*

27

She continued, 'And even granddad's youngest sister, my great-aunt Phyllis who brought mother up, spoke Zulu so well that she would correct her young Zulu servants. She would say, "That is not the way to speak. You have a beautiful language and you must speak it correctly." I remember one servant asked whether he should bring *isobho*, meaning the gravy. Well, auntie got so angry that she nearly flung him out of the dining-room. She said, "*Umhluzi, umhluzi*, the juice that runs from the meat, gravy, not *isobho*."'[6]

After he left school, Marwick recorded the highlights of his school years.[7] Like schoolchildren everywhere, the Richmond schoolchildren tried every trick to skip class. Going for a drink of water was tried as an escape. 'Each child possessed a drinking can or pannikin, and at intervals of about fifteen minutes each would apply for and obtain permission to quench his or her thirst at the neighbouring well.' The teacher put a stop to these continuous trips to the well by giving a few children a hiding and eventually by refusing any child permission to go to the well.

One important event in the school which Marwick remembered was the retirement and farewell of Mr T Kearsley, the head teacher. The children collected money to buy him a farewell gift. 'When the inevitable breaking-up day arrived we assembled in the old room with proud hearts to witness the presentation of a price of sovereigns and an escritour [sic] to our much respected master ... At the close of breaking-up celebrations the members of our senior class went forward and one of them having made a suitable address presented the gifts on behalf of the schoolchildren with their best wishes for Mr Kearsley's happiness in retirement.'

Marwick remembered that at one time, during a severe thunderstorm, the roof of the schoolhouse – made of thatch and poles – blew off. Luckily no one was hurt and only a few books were damaged. However, the men in the village got together to see to the construction of not only a new roof, but later a whole new school. It had a boarding school for boys as well as girls. The new primary school opened after the Christmas holidays in 1884.

Mr W J Hedgcock replaced Mr Kearsley as the new principal – no longer the head teacher – and changed the rules and regulations at the newly-built school. There were rules about when to go to the toilet, when to get water and where the boundaries of the playground were. Hedgcock also introduced military drill for the older boys. Like boys elsewhere in the colony, like real soldiers, they were taught to be disciplined, to endure hardship and to obey orders.

Sport formed an important part of the school and community. The young Marwicks were runners and won many trophies. Clare Rossouw recalled a story which her grandfather had told them about his childhood. It was one of their favourite stories: 'There was going to be a sports day in Richmond. One of the farmers' wives decided that, as a prize, she was going to make a tart as big as an ox-wagon wheel. It was to be filled with her own apricot jam. So on the side, where all the running was happening, was this huge tart that was going to be given to the best runner. And said granddad, "Jimmy James Pee Payn Hackland, his name was James Hackland, was longing to win this, but he was a little fat boy. Still he was hoping to win it."

'At the end of the day, when they were choosing the best runners of the day, they chose uncle Rob and my granddad. The tart was to go to Rob and Sidney. And they could see that poor little James Hackland was terribly disappointed and they did not want this huge cartwheel full of jam.

'They said to him, "You have it." Little James could not believe it.

'And granddad said, "He just got down and started licking the jam and he just kept on licking and licking."

'One or two of them said to him, "You mustn't eat too much of that." But he took no notice. And then, suddenly, he gave a loud groan and held his stomach: "Oh, *we ma me? We ma me, ngiyafa, ngiyafa,* I'm dying, I'm dying."

'And Rob and Sidney got a fright and ran home, and got their father's wheelbarrow. They ran back to the showgrounds where the races had taken place. They loaded James Hackland into the wheelbarrow and then they ran all the way to his mother's house with him in the wheelbarrow jogging along, because they were terrified that they were going to be accused of killing this kid. We loved that story, we used to ask granddad to tell the story over and over again.'

A studio photograph of the young Sid Marwick and his brother Alan. These young men hiked from Richmond to Pietermaritzburg one night to test their fluency in the Zulu language in the company of a group of unknown Zulus.
Many years later Alan awaited his brother at Pietermaritzburg station after the completion of the long march. *(Courtesy Killie Campbell Africana Library)*

After he left school Marwick still competed in sporting activities. In 1893 in Pietermaritzburg he was presented with a silver tray. It was engraved, 'Trial stakes won by J S Marwick, 1893'.[8]

Running was not the only sport in Richmond. It was traditionally accepted that the settler men began playing cricket in the village as early as 1852. A Richmond Lawn Tennis Club was founded in 1876, a year after Sidney was born.

More and more children attended the school, school inspectors arrived to inspect what was done at the school and exams were written each November. From 1888 school prizes were awarded annually. Overall the Marwick children did well. The school grew so big that Miss Hedgcock, the principal's sister who had arrived from England, was appointed as the assistant teacher to teach the younger children.

There was new work to be learnt. All the children had great trouble in learning how the English money system worked. Twelve pence equalled one shilling; twenty shillings equalled one pound. When a boy gave an incorrect answer to a sum, 'the Master responded with a resounding whack and an audible titter greeted the discomfiture of this youthful aspirant to honour. In an effort to justify himself ... he offered the lame excuse of "Please, sir, it's not in my book."' Marwick recalled that the unlucky boy who got the answer wrong was called 'Irish', the equivalent in those days of being rather unintelligent!

In 1893, five years after they left school, Marwick also recorded what had happened to his schoolfriends. Now aged between eighteen and twenty, they had chosen very different careers ranging from farming and business to studying overseas at the University of Edinburgh in Scotland. 'Lawrence Allsop and Leonard Link are at present in Durban Merchant's houses, Rob and Sid Marwick are clerks in the Secretary of Native Affairs Office in Pietermaritzburg, Frank Mercy and Isabel Brickhill are residing in Weenen county, Arthur Jackson is farming at Upper Umzimkulu, Kenyan Howden is pursuing his studies at Edinburgh College [sic] and Harry Butten is in the Transvaal, while the remainder still reside in the locality of Richmond.' These immigrant children had received a good education at the village school, based on sound Scottish principles. They had grown up in a close-knit English-speaking community with strong links to their mother country, Great Britain. In many cases these young people, when they grew up, had married members of neighbouring families. And by Marwick's account, many of them supported and served their adopted country well.

Chapter 3

THE ZULU MEN WHO WENT TO THE WITWATERSRAND

1890–1899

Conditions in rural Zululand and Natal were difficult in the early 1890s. The long drought which began in 1888 lasted until 1893. In October 1893 and again in 1894 locusts arrived in swarms two and a half kilometres wide, taking more than an hour and a half to pass over-head. In 1896 the crop was almost half of what it had been the year before. In 1897 a further disaster struck when rinderpest broke out in Zululand and Natal, as it did in many other parts of southern Africa. This highly contagious cattle disease caused animals to contract a fever and die within a week. In 1897 the rinderpest struck at a time when the cattle were young and very vulnerable, and herds died in great numbers.

A few head of cattle in front of a Zulu hut. Herds in Zululand were badly depleted when a disastrous rinderpest epidemic struck southern Africa in 1897. Many young Zulu men were sent to earn money on the gold-fields in order to restock the herds. *(Courtesy Transnet Heritage Library)*

Chiefs of the Mbomvu and men from the Ganya chiefdom decided to send the young men of their clans to the gold-fields so that they could earn money to buy grain and cattle. Men from Ixopo, the Upper Umkomazi and the Kranzkop districts who were already on the Witwatersrand sent money home to feed their hungry relatives. Even though hours were long and work on the mines was hard and dangerous, wages on the gold-fields were much better than in Natal. In the 1890s wages on the mines rose from 42s. to 63s. 6d. per month. In addition, mine-owners needed workers so badly that they were willing to accept workers on very short contracts. And the Natal government itself was very happy for its people to go to work on the gold-fields – it hoped that most of the money earned there would return to Natal.

Mining houses sent labour agents or touts to Zululand and Natal to recruit workers for the mines. An agent would arrive at a kraal to negotiate with the clan chiefs how many young men (including boys as young as twelve) would be sent to the mines and how much they would earn. Local traders in the rural areas also recruited young men to work on the mines. In order to tempt them, traders in Zululand would give a young man a cash advance or cattle before he left for the Rand. In return, a man would work for very low wages on the mines. When a worker signed up, he committed himself to repaying the advance he had received. Traders themselves benefited because mine-owners, to whom they sent the workers, paid 20s. to 30s. for each prospective miner who arrived on the gold-fields.

Before the railway line was completed between Durban and Charlestown, across the ZAR border from Volksrust, in 1893, anyone who wanted to travel to the gold-fields had to go on horseback, by wagon, coach or cart, or on foot. Like other workers, most Zulus walked from Natal to the Witwatersrand. It was a long and dangerous journey. Often a farmer over whose land they walked would catch them and force them to work for him in return for their passage through his land. Sometimes they would be caught and fined by men pretending to be policemen. At other times they would be attacked by bandits or by wild animals. Often the men would run out of food on the road and would arrive half starved on the Witwatersrand, too weak to work. If the mine-owners did not feed them or give them time to regain their strength, they would not be able to work.

Mine-owners needed every able-bodied male who arrived on the Rand. In 1889, three years after the discovery of gold, some 10 000 black men worked on the diggings. In 1893, when mining companies began to sink shafts to follow the gold reef deeper underground, they employed 29 000 men. By 1896, more than 70 000 miners worked on the gold-fields as the mines went even deeper. By 1899 there were 97 000 black men working on the mines.

Workers were able to choose the length of their contract. Although six months was the usual period of time, sometimes men were able to sign up for only one

One of the biggest compounds on the Rand was at the New Primrose Gold Mining Company. It housed some 3 000 mineworkers. The pitched-roof buildings in the centre were the kitchens. The hospital and the office of the compound manager were located on the right. (*Courtesy Johannesburg College of Education Library*)

month. In addition, if miners heard that working conditions at another mine were better than at the one they had been contracted to, very often, after they were paid at one mine, they left for another. Although black miners needed passes to move from one employer to another and were fined if they had no passes, employers were happy to pay the fines of their new workers.

At first mine-owners did not provide their workers with a place to stay. Only after 1890 did mine-owners begin to build compounds for their workers. These were wood and iron barracks, often without windows and with earth floors. These sleeping quarters faced inward, around a square, where there would be a cook house as well as the administration building.

Compounds housed between 400 and 600 men. The miners were free to come and go as they pleased, but needed a travel pass once they wanted to leave the prop-

erty of the mine. They were not greatly bothered with these passes. There were not enough policemen to enforce either the law on travel passes or the law which required workers to carry a pass stating who their employers were.

Miners in the compounds were creative businessmen in their own way. Many had sidelines which enabled them to make extra money while they were on the goldfields. Some sold food or firewood that was very scarce on the highveld where few trees were found. Some made bracelets or musical instruments from copper, iron wire or other materials that they had stolen at work. Other men stole iron files which they reforged at home and iron piping which was used to make stills in which to distil liquor. Many white supervisors who had worked in mines overseas turned a blind eye to this kind of theft. These miners believed that it was one of the perks of the job. The theft of gold was, however, punished severely.

Life on the Witwatersrand gold-fields was hard and dangerous. Mining accidents were varied and frequent: miners were injured or even killed by rockfalls, collapsing shafts, falling cages, ladders and other objects. They were crushed by trams, drowned in flooded passages, suffocated by gases and smoke in the tunnels underground, or blown up by explosions which went wrong when poor quality explosives were used. Statistics on fatal accidents were kept for the first time in 1893. It was calculated that for every one thousand black miners, nearly six died in accidents. In 1896 the figure was slightly lower: almost five deaths per one thousand miners. In comparison only 1,6 deaths per thousand due to mining accidents were recorded in England during the same period.

Working under such dangerous conditions and having to depend on others to do their jobs properly, black miners preferred to work with men whom they knew or who came from their home towns or villages. Most Zulus worked above ground, while black miners from Mozambique became drillers or hammer boys, the most dangerous jobs on the mines.

Scores of young men who migrated to the Rand in search of work were often little more than children. Many very young boys were used to work the narrow and difficult stopes underground, not only because they were small, but because they could be paid less and were easier to train and to discipline. Only in 1896 did a new law prohibit boys under the age of twelve from working underground. No such restriction existed for work on the surface. The employment of boys under

Young Zulu miners busy loading gold ore into small cocopans to be taken to the stamp batteries at the Stanhope Gold Mining Company. Most of the young men are wearing western-style clothes and hats according to the custom of the time. *(Courtesy Rare Book Collection, Rand Afrikaans University: Library Services)*

34

twelve on the coal mines in Great Britain had been stopped in 1887, not even ten years earlier.

The young boys worked with and shared their living quarters with seasoned and experienced miners who were their elders. On the mines strong bonds developed between the older men and boys. Older men kept boys as *izinkotshane* or boy-wives who had to perform traditional wifely duties such as fetching water, cooking food, running errands or any other odd jobs. In 1898 a Swiss missionary, Henri-Alexandre Junod, wrote of the existence of so-called 'immoral customs' in the mine compounds. It is perhaps a reference to the early practice of *ubukhontxana* or mine marriages between adult and younger men which developed on the mines in the twentieth century.[1]

On the mines, miners not only had to survive accidents, but illnesses as well. In1893/4 and in 1897/8, smallpox epidemics killed thousands of workers. Dysentery and typhoid, diseases caused by overcrowding and unsanitary conditions, sometimes reached almost epidemic proportions. In winter pneumonia killed even more men. In 1890 almost thirty-one men out of every thousand living on the gold-fields died of pneumonia. In 1893/4 thirty-five men out of every thousand died; in very cramped and overcrowded conditions this figure increased to forty-two. After 1895 new laws were passed to force mine-owners to build their own hospitals. Very few did this, however. The only hospital on the Rand was Johannesburg Hospital, which was too far for most black miners to go to. In addition, the hospital was reserved mainly for whites.

Very few black women came to the gold-fields in the early days. In 1896 there were only 1 678 black women on the Rand, of which only two per cent were married. This meant that there was only one woman for every sixty-three men; in fact, there was only one woman between the ages of twenty-five and thirty-nine for every ninety-eight men. Most of these women lived in the backyards on the properties of white people where they worked as domestic servants, or did washing and ironing work. Some women lived in shacks on vacant plots of land in town. Only very few women lived in the small villages which sprang up on mine property. Here many brewed beer, something they had learnt to do long before they came to the gold-fields. The women who brewed and sold beer to miners who came to their drinking places for company often became prostitutes. With so few women on the gold-fields, venereal disease spread rapidly.

There were not many leisure activities available for young black workers. Some went to church, others went to eating houses and canteens, or became involved in fights with miners from other mines. By 1895 there were sixty-five volunteer preachers in the black locations of Johannesburg, Jeppestown, Krugersdorp and Boksburg. Many preachers also visited the compounds at the Langlaagte, Simmer and Jack, New Primrose and George Goch mines. On Sundays in the compounds one could hear church brass bands playing or loud hymn-singing, accompanied by the harmonium or accordion.

Many workers met their friends at local eating houses. Sitting on long benches, they could share a meal. A slice of bread and a plate of soup cost 3d., a slice of bread and a serving of meat cost 6d., and bread, meat and coffee was 9d. The daily meal in the mine compounds consisted of cooked maize meal. Each group of men would then add their own food – especially meat – to the meal.

Before the sale of alcohol to black people was prohibited in 1897, workers would meet in canteens. These were open from six o'clock in the morning until nine o'clock at night. Between 1888 and 1895 the number of licensed bars on the Witwatersrand increased from 147 to 1 000. This meant that there was one bar for every sixty men on the Rand. On their days off, on Saturday and Sunday, most workers would visit these bars which made huge profits by selling them very dangerous mixtures of alcohol. It was said that one tot at 6d. was enough, two enough to make you drunk and three to make you blind drunk.

The weekend drinking took its toll. Mine-owners calculated that about a quarter or a third of their entire workforce were absent from work every Monday and most of Tuesday, suffering from massive hangovers. It was also said that drunkenness caused most of the accidents on the mines. Mine-owners hoped that the 1897 law would help to get more workers to work on Mondays. Missionaries and churches supported mine-owners in this law. They said that Sunday was the most notorious and dangerous day all along the Witwatersrand.

Sundays were indeed dangerous. Fights would break out, often with anything between 500 and 1 000 men on each side. The men would fight using knobkerries, stones, assegais, broken bottles, shovels, picks, drills or any other weapon they could lay their hands on. These developed from the ways of fighting that many had learned as boys in the rural areas. There they had learnt to settle differences with boys of other neighbouring age regiments in wild stick-fights.

One of the biggest faction fights ever recorded on the Witwatersrand, began on Monday 7 October 1895 as a canteen brawl. Soon Zulus, Shangaans, Chopis and Inhambanes met in an open space between the Geldenhuys and Jumpers mines. Eventually two to three thousand men fought on each side. They took shelter behind the stone embankments of the tram-lines and used the stone as ammunition. That day the Zulu side was defeated by the Shangaans and a number of men were killed.

Hardship and even death awaited black miners on the gold-fields. Yet most prepared to return home after a six-month contract. Miners would sometimes go to the general dealer on the mine, early in their stay, where they bought a trunk. As they earned more money they would fill the trunk with things which they wanted to take home with them. From hawkers miners purchased what they thought would impress the people at home: items that their parents considered luxuries, such as watches to measure time and pens with which to write – an important skill in a society where very few people were literate. They bought western-style clothes: vests, waistcoats, shirts, jackets, socks, boots and belts. They bought brushes and combs, spoons, bedspreads, tablecloths, blankets, mirrors and cloth. They also took knives and iron files which they could reforge at home.

At the end of his contract a miner would settle his debt with the general dealer, claim his trunk and set off home with perhaps as much as £15 in savings. Whether or not a returning miner sent money home via a bank, he still stood a good chance of being robbed of his small change. Then, having arrived home, he would have to pay

taxes to his chief and hut tax. Afterwards a miner would hand out gifts and buy beer and food to celebrate his home-coming as well as his status as a miner. Indeed, going to the mines, just before the end of the century, had become an important part of a young man's initiation into the world of mature men.

Zulu men on the Witwatersrand who did not want to work on the mines found respectable and very well-paid work in other spheres. It was calculated that on the eve of the Anglo-Boer War there were almost 30 000 black people employed as domestic servants, cooks, messengers, washermen, brickmakers, grooms and municipal workers. Often young Zulus found work as domestic servants in the homes of white miners who had brought

Workers on their way home after a stint on the gold-fields. Most men walked back loaded with as much as they could comfortably carry. At night the blankets around their shoulders probably served as bedding. *(Courtesy MuseuMAfricA)*

their families to Johannesburg. At first, while still inexperienced, they were called 'kitchenboys'. They made fires, cleaned stoves, swept the house and the yard and kept them clean, prepared the morning and afternoon tea, and weeded and watered the garden. After more training, they became 'houseboys'. Houseboys prepared or helped to prepare and serve meals, and even served their employers their early morning coffee in the bedroom. They would also act as coachmen; their job then was to look after the horse and trap when their mistresses went shopping in downtown Johannesburg.

Houseboys were often on duty from between five and seven o'clock in the morning until six or nine o'clock at night. During the afternoon they had a few hours off before they began to prepare the evening meal. In addition, they usually had the day off on Sunday when they went to visit their friends in the mine compounds or in other black locations along the Reef. They would go walking in suburbs like Jeppe, dressed in 'the most up-to-date costumes and carrying canes and sticks, swaggering along using English language of the most appalling description'.[2]

Houseboys were paid in cash, but also received board and lodging. Their meals consisted of some of the food that they prepared for the family in addition to mealie meal for porridge and cheap cuts of meat. They slept in small rooms in the backyard or in the stables, if the house where they worked was grand enough. Where no room was available, they often slept on the kitchen floor.

Soon after the discovery of gold, members of a guild of washermen, the *AmaWasha*, came to the gold-fields from towns such as Durban or Pietermaritzburg to ply their trade and do washing for the thousands of white miners who were flooding to the Rand. Men from the rural district of Umsinga as well as from the Kanyile, Vilikazi, Sithole, Mchunu and Buthelezi clans in Zululand grabbed the opportunity to make money. They very often brought their young sons with them as their mat bearers and began to train them to become washermen.

The first washermen arrived on the Rand in 1890. Three years later, 700 men were plying this trade. By 1896 there were 1 200 *AmaWasha* on the Rand.

The *AmaWasha* who rented land along the Braamfontein Spruit built a series of small dams in the spruit in which to do their washing. As one dam followed another along the spruit, the dirty water of one dam flowed into the next – in which more washing was done. It was not a very hygienic way of washing clothes at the best of times. During the drought of 1895 the situation became so bad that Johannesburg health inspectors closed the site at Braamfontein until such time as these dams had been properly cleaned.

The *AmaWasha* usually collected their fees for the previous week's washing and new bundles of dirty washing on Mondays. One washerman could usually wash about three bundles of clothes a day or eighteen bundles a week. At four shillings a bundle a washerman earned about £3 per week or £12 per month. It was a very good wage at the time. Some

The *AmaWasha*, a guild of Zulu washermen, did the laundry of many of the single miners who lived in boarding houses close to the mines on the Reef. The washing was done at sites outside the town – at Braamfontein, Elandsfontein, Booysens and Concordia – where small spruits rose in the hills. These spruits gave the area its name: Witwatersrand, 'ridge of white waters'. *(Courtesy Rare Book Collection, Rand Afrikaans University: Library Services)*

washermen earned even more money by selling items of clothing stolen from the bundles of laundry which they had been given to wash. Overall, a Zulu who spent two four-month periods on the Rand as one of the *AmaWasha* could return home with as much as £80 to £100. In rural Natal people regarded a man who earned this kind of money as a rich man.

Along the spruit the men built some wood and iron huts where they lived and one hut in which they could store their bundles of washing overnight. At the Sans Souci washing site along the Braamfontein Spruit, where about eighty washermen lived, they planted their own crops and kept a few cattle, pigs and a horse to pull their carts. These washing sites were governed according to Nguni custom. A high-ranking *induna* controlled the washermen, organised a watch to see that washing was not stolen by others and usually accepted only people he knew to fill vacancies amongst the washermen. Once a month the washermen, in the age sets with which they had grown up, would march into town to renew their washermen's licences, 'keeping perfect time' and singing the old songs of their regiments. Then they would gather on Market Square in the centre of Johannesburg to discuss their business and pay their respects to their leader, Kwaaiman (literally, 'tough man').[3]

The Witwatersrand gold-fields provided ways to make money lawfully. It also

39

offered great opportunities for highway-men, robbers and petty thieves. Robbers could earn easy money by waylaying workers on their way to and from the Rand. In 1890 it was estimated that nearly three thousand workers walked to the Rand each month.

Most of the Zulu-speaking petty thieves and criminals, called *izigebengu*, lived in the Klipriviersberg hills just south of Johannesburg, close to the road leading to Natal. Some 200 men, women and children lived in the kloofs and caves at a place called Shabalawawa. Their leader, a man called Nohlopa, came from Kwabe in Zululand. However, after a stint in jail, Nohlopa converted to Christianity and became a preacher and a fellow Zulu, who took the name of Jan Note, took over the leadership of the band and formed it into the *Umkosi Wezintaba* – the Regiment of the Hills. This well-organised band of criminals became very successful highway robbers. But they did not operate only on the highways. Newspapers in Johannesburg also complained about a gang of well-organised 'Zulus' who were committing a large number of burglaries in the town.[4]

Whether the men earned a living on the mines, in the kitchens, at the spruits or on the highways of the Witwatersrand, their stay on the gold-fields changed them forever. In 1895 Mr H W Boast, the resident magistrate at Kranskop, approved of the men who returned: 'When they return to their kraals, whatever they may do elsewhere, they certainly behave themselves, and, so far I have no cause to complain of natives getting into demoralised habits by working at the Transvaal gold-fields. I find

too, that once a Native has been to the Gold Fields, he is not keen to return and prefers to work in Natal for a moderate wage. The same remark applies to Natives from Zululand, I believe.'[5]

The magistrate of the Upper Umkomanzi Division, Mr A Morking, disagreed: 'Going to the Gold Fields does not in any way improve Natives, as when they return they will not work for wages given in the Colony, having received treble the amount at the Gold Fields, which amount the Natal farmers are unable to pay.' Mr D G Giles, magistrate of the Upper Tugela Division, was equally disapproving. 'The moral condition of Natives in this Division is by no means improving by contact with Johannesburg, and is showing itself in many ways. They are fast becoming as untruthful a lot as I ever came in contact with.'[6] The magistrate at Ndwandwe also said of the young men who went to Johannesburg that they 'have latterly taken to squandering their earnings and staying at the Rand instead of saving and coming home with the [money] for the use of their families'.[7]

We have no idea, unfortunately, what their elders thought of these young men who returned from the gold-fields once they had completed a six- to eight-month contract on the mines. We hear only about fathers looking for their sons. In 1899 the magistrate at Nongoma remarked that some young men 'left their kraal some years ago and have never remitted any money nor have they ever visited home. Their father is much concerned about their conduct and [is] getting old.'[8]

Chapter 4

THE FIRST NATAL NATIVE AGENT IN JOHANNESBURG

1895–1899

When he left school in 1888 young Marwick could choose one of a number of careers. He could go into business, become a government official or a farmer. He could study medicine or law overseas – if his family was able to afford to send him there – or, like his friend Harry Butten, he could try his luck on the gold-fields. Marwick chose to begin a career in the office of the Secretary of Native Affairs of the Colony of Natal.

Marwick's ascent of the bureaucratic ladder began at the bottom. In 1892 he became the acting clerk and interpreter at the regional magistrate's court of the Lower Umzimkulu Division. After a month he moved to the Alfred Division where, in addition to his duties, he became a sub-distributor of stamps at the court as well as the deputy clerk of the peace.

From November 1892 until August 1893 young Marwick remained in the same position, but was moved to the Lions River Division and the Upper Umkomanzi Division. In September he was posted to the Durban magistrate's court for six months. In April 1894 he was again sent to the platteland to serve in the Upper Umkomanzi Division and at the magistrate's office in New Hanover.

'I was also studying to pass the necessary exams in the Native language before Mr Justice Shepstone KCMG as a sworn Zulu Interpreter and Translator of the Supreme Court in March 1895,' Marwick himself reported.[1] As sworn translator he would be able to translate all official legal documents and act as interpreter in court cases.

According to Marwick's granddaughter, Clare Rossouw, 'Granddad and his younger brother Alan wanted to be accredited as interpreters. They said to themselves, "We must make sure that our Zulu is good enough. We mustn't assume just that because we have grown up talking Zulu, that we are good enough."

'One evening, when there was no moon,

41

MS
MAR
2·08'

131
1895

MOTIONS

In the Supreme Court of the Colony of Natal.

In the matter of

An application by
John Sydney Marwick
for admission as a sworn
Interpreter and Translator of
this Honourable Court in the
English and Zulu languages

It is ordered
That the Applicant the said John Sydney
Marwick, he and he is hereby admitted
as a sworn Interpreter and Translator of
this Honourable Court in the English and
Zulu languages.
Exd.   (sgd.) W. Broome
                         Registrar.

A True Copy
Jor (Johnson)
Registrar + L.R.M

they waited in the dark at the side of the Maritzburg-Richmond road. They heard a group of young men walking and they called out and said, "Can we join you?"

'And these men said, "Come, come." And they walked and they walked and as it got light, these men were absolutely horrified. They said, "*Hawu, abelungu.*" They hadn't realised that the two new-comers were white people. All night long they had been walking along making jokes, talking about their white bosses and using very idiomatic, very fluent Zulu. They hadn't picked up that either granddad or Alan was white. And grand-dad and Alan said, "We are definitely qualified. We can go and apply to be interpreters." And so they did, and became recognised interpreters. But granddad was always a perfectionist.'[2]

Above: On 12 March 1899 Marwick was appointed as a sworn translator of English and Zulu at the Supreme Court of the Colony of Natal. (*Courtesy Killie Campbell Africana Library*) Right: The young Marwick. This photograph was taken in Pietermaritzburg, possibly before his departure to Johannesburg to become the first Natal Native Agent on the Rand. (*Courtesy Clare Rossouw*)

Marwick's training served him well. He climbed the bureaucratic ladder steadily. In January 1895 he became a Third Class Clerk in Pietermaritzburg, the capital of the colony of Natal. In October 1895, having demonstrated his abilities, he was transferred to Johannesburg as the acting representative of the Department of the Secretary for Native Affairs in Natal at their newly opened office. In February 1896 Marwick was given more responsibility when he became the Native Agent for Zululand as well. In August 1897 he was appointed as the fully fledged representative of the Department. Although native agents were a common sight in the countryside of Natal, it was the first time that the Natal government had appointed a native agent to look after the interest of the black workers from Natal outside the borders of the colony.

Before his departure from Pietermaritzburg, his colleagues presented Marwick with a farewell gift of a set of gold studs and a nugget pin. 'Mr Marwick carries with him the good wishes of all his colleagues and a large circle of friends,' concluded the local newspaper.[3]

At the time of his appointment in Johannesburg, Marwick was only twenty years old. He had, however, been in Johannesburg before.

'When he was still very young,' remembers his granddaughter Clare, 'he took over the job of transporting goods to the Reef from his elder brother, James. He never went back to school again. None of the Marwicks stayed at school very long.'

In October 1895 during an interview

This photograph of Johannesburg was taken from the hill behind Doornfontein. During the 1890s it was one of the affluent suburbs in the growing city where many mine-owners built their mansions. Some of these can be seen in the foreground. (*Courtesy Johannesburg College of Education Library*)

with the daily newspaper *The Star* in Johannesburg, Marwick recalled the visit when he was only fifteen years old: 'This is not my first experience of Johannesburg, nor am I altogether devoid of previous experience in the peculiar duties of my new office. Five years ago, I came to the Rand in charge of a party of Natal natives sent up under contract for the May Consolidated Mining Company. During the time I was in Johannesburg I had a great deal to do in the way of keeping up communication between my natives and their friends. That, of course, was simply done in a private way and with the object of keeping our natives contented. As they were all under one contract it was a comparatively easy thing to do. As long as a native knows his friends are all right, that is all he wants,' he added rather patronisingly.

The reporter of the Johannesburg newspaper the *Standard and Diggers'* *News*, who also interviewed Marwick, was not quite convinced that this confident, inexperienced young man from Natal would be able to do the job he had been appointed to do. He commented that Marwick 'with the ingenuousness of youth has told all that we wanted to know'. Without knowing much about conditions in Johannesburg, Marwick very naively told the newspaper: 'I have no doubt whatever that I shall be able to show that, in the majority of cases of alleged robbery or fraud, the boys have themselves invented the stories to explain the smallness of their money earnings, the deficiency of which is really caused by their own spending at the mines.'

Young Marwick had grown up in rural Richmond, had experienced life in the rural areas of Natal, knew Pietermaritzburg and had spent six months in Durban, and had visited Johannesburg once before. He still had a lot to learn

This general view along the line of the main gold reef shows the works of the May Consolidated Mining Company on the left, and those of the Glencairn Company on the right. On the left a small blue-gum plantation is visible. The timber from these fast-growing Australian trees was used extensively in the mines to support the incline stopes. (*Courtesy Johannesburg College of Education Library*)

about the city and the kind of people who made up this new mining town. It was a tough place where gold was king and where many people made money by lying, stealing or cheating. The newspaper could not resist making fun of his statement. 'To put it plainly, the service which Mr Marwick's appointment will have rendered will be to have proved the honesty of Johannesburg people and the rascality of the Natal native who goes there to seek employment.'

Marwick needed to prove not only that he could do a good job for one so young, but also that the post to which he had been appointed had been worth creating. A letter published in the *Natal Witness* was very critical of Marwick's appointment. 'What will be the agent's occupation? He cannot act as legal advisor, he has no status in the Transvaal, and he cannot act as arbitrator for he is assumed to be the protector of the natives ... If the agent lays himself out as a friend and adviser of the natives who are employed at the mines he will very soon find himself in conflict with both ... No good can possibly now arise from this appointment.'

Another letter writer defended Marwick's appointment in Johannesburg and better understood the plight of Zulu workers in Johannesburg. 'Natal natives have been in the habit of going to work in "eGoli" for many years past, and frequently with deplorable consequences ... At present many men who leave for the gold-fields are as effectively lost to their families and friends as if they had gone to sea and been shipwrecked. The more

respectable men who return are imbued with a lively horror of the place, and do all they can to prevent their younger relatives going there ... I know of at least one instance (having been called in to explain the Dutch money orders) where money has been sent pretty regularly to a man's wife. Those who know the difficulties of life at the mines – even for white men – will appreciate what this means; and when boys who can neither read nor write, and know nothing of postal arrangements, know that they can hand over their wages to Mr Marwick and communicate with their families through him, the number of such cases is likely to be largely increased.'[4]

Regardless of these differences of opinion in Natal, Marwick set to work to carry out his instructions. He was assisted by G D Wheelwright and H B Wallace as well as by two Zulu messengers known only as Mqanjelwa and Manase, who had to contact miners in locations and compounds along the Reef.

The Native Agent's office was open from 7.30 in the morning until 6.30 in the evening. Marwick and his colleagues saw a great many people. In 1897 alone, 20 615 Zulus from Zululand and Natal had registered at the pass office in Johannesburg, most of whom would have known about the office at 61 Marshall Street. When Zulus visited the office, 'they voluntarily conform to their standard of good manners in the office, and are allowed to state their business in their usual way, that is, while sitting on the ground,' Marwick explained.

Marwick described his work. 'Until the

A studio photograph of Marwick (right) and his colleague, Guy Wheelwright, who managed the Germiston branch of the Natal Native Agency and who accompanied Marwick on the march. *(Courtesy Killie Campbell Africana Library)*

6th of October 1899, I was employed in the work at Johannesburg – my duties were to bank, and, if desired, to remit Natives' earnings to Natal, to give advice and assistance to Natives subjected to injustice, to assist Natives destitute and in sickness, or who had been injured in the Mines. The official records will show that, during the four years I was so employed, the sum of £134,000 was remitted to Natal, hundreds of cases of injustice were represented annually to the Transvaal officials, and money grants were obtained from the Gold Mining Companies for Natives permanently disabled through mining accidents.'

Besides helping to send money home,

Marwick's office also issued Zulu workers with train tickets to return to Natal.[5] During 1897 the office issued 13 016 train tickets to the value of £23,392 13s.6d. Whenever a ticket was issued, the person was warned that he would have to catch the train on the date for which the ticket was bought, or the ticket would be invalid. Men who could neither read nor write were often cheated by railway officials who did not give them the correct change. The Netherlands South Africa Railway Company (NZASM) introduced a new system. Marwick explained, 'Tickets now issued have been printed with a number of round dots on the back denoting the amount of railway fare, and a Native is thereby enabled to judge whether he has been duped or not: for example the railway fare to Richmond Road (£2 1s. 6d.) is expressed by means of calculi thus: OO 0 o.'

Some years later, Marwick looked back on the work he had done. 'When I arrived in Johannesburg, an important part of my work was to help the men from Natal who had not received their wages or had been cheated out of their wages.' In 1897 alone his office handled 833 complaints of wages which had been withheld.

He continued, 'On a Native making an affidavit before the official referred to, the complainant's employer is warned to appear before the Landdrost on a given date, and an enquiry into the merits of the complaint is made under the provisions of the Master's and Servant's Act. In some cases, Natives return to report that the amount of wages claimed has been recovered, but such cases bear only a small ratio to the number of complaints preferred at this office.'

Marwick added that in 1897, 'at the instance of 180 Zulus, assisted by this office, a European was convicted during September last of withholding wages amounting to £826 1s. 6d. and was sentenced to pay a fine of £100 or to undergo imprisonment for three months with hard labour.

'Cases in which Transvaal officials defrauded Natives were investigated by our office, and, when there was sufficient evidence, prosecutions were instituted. As a result of our exposure of systematic frauds practised upon Natives by Town Council employees the Press demanded the dismissal of two prominent officials of the Council in August 1899.'

Each week Marwick visited the native wards of the Johannesburg Hospital to record whether any Zulus from Natal had died. He would then inform their relatives at home.

'I did not find that many men in hospital,' Marwick said. 'Numbers of natives, on sickening with fever or pneumonia, prefer to be tended by their friends in their rough sleeping quarters rather than submit to being taken to Hospital. They regard the railway as a more influential factor than the Hospital in "lessening the sum of human suffering".' He was referring to the fact that more people preferred to go home by train than to go to hospital.

In 1897 Marwick sent £27 000 to Natal. Of this, only £7 800 was sent to white people. The rest was sent to Zulu chiefs and relatives on mission stations in Natal and Zululand.

In 1897 '£1,300 was sent to Chief Kula in the Umsinga district, £526 to Chief Homoi in the Krantzkop district, £166 to the Edendale Mission Station in the Umgeni district, £22 to the Amanzimtoti Mission Station, up to the meagre £2 which was sent to Chief Bikwayo in the Umlazi district,' Marwick concluded. The list was three pages long.

Marwick explained why some men sent home more money than others. 'Many men sent home money in order to buy cattle for *lobola* or for breeding purposes. Others sent home money to repay loans or contributed money towards building a church or to pay the legal expenses in cases where the chieftainship was disputed. During 1897 £96 was sent to the Amanzimtoti Mission Station, £50 to the Impolweni Mission Station and £45 to the Georgedale Mission.'

Marwick provided detailed information on who sent money home: 'The people under Kula, grandson of Majozi, erstwhile *induna* of the late Sir Theophilus Shepstone, KCMG, have entrusted large proportions of their earnings to us. This could be attributed to the continuance of that confidence in things Governmental which was won from them by the wisdom and personality of the deceased statesman, to whom their very existence as a tribe is due.

'Those men who live on private lands have to pay high rents and repay heavy loans, with punctuality, hence their frequent remittances through this office,' Marwick continued. 'The tribesmen referred to, command the highest wages paid to Native domestic servants on the

Rand, their characteristics being intelligence and habits of cleanliness and industry.' But Marwick went on to criticise these men. 'They are, withal, imitative and impulsive, and their capability for superior service to that of their fellow natives seems but too often to result in their acquiring a taste for liquor, which, in turn, acts as an incentive to criminality.

'Then there were Mandulini's men. They were often engaged in surface work on the mining properties, and are also to be found in service within the limits of the town. Some of them are purchasers of Crown Lands in Natal and often remit money to Natal through us.'

Zulus who worked on the surface at the mines sorted the ore. At revolving tables where the ore was deposited, they picked out the valueless pieces of rock which contained no gold-bearing pebbles. The men then put the sorted ore through a crusher. Small pieces of ore passed through the stamp battery where they were reduced to finely crushed rock. When this rock was treated chemically, the gold could be recovered.[6]

Other Zulus found work at the town council of Johannesburg.

'Bhekukupiwa's men, who have interests – including the purchase of Crown Lands – in common with those of Mandulini, are employed in less congenial occupations. They are, almost exclusively, engaged on the Sanitary Service of the Town Council, removing the night soil of the town. The filthy habits and felonious proclivities of this tribe (the AmaBaca) betoken its members to be the veritable Pariahs of the Natal Native population, and their nightly thefts from the sleeping Johannesburger are not less frequent than are their depredations on the flocks of the Ixopo sheep farmer,' Marwick exclaimed. 'But Natives engaged on the Sanitary Service are well paid,' he added.

Like the rest of Johannesburg, Marwick did not much like the AmaBaca who removed the buckets from the out-houses of Johannesburg at night. He thought that they were extremely dirty and that they had petty criminal tendencies which they had not picked up in Johannesburg, but had acquired in their home district of Ixopo where they had the reputation of being stock thieves.

Zulu women also sent money home. Like other black women on the Rand, many resorted to beer brewing and prostitution in order to survive, and to send money home. In 1897 Marwick reported to his head office: 'There is an appalling number of Natal native women of the *nondindwa* class on the Rand at the present time. The ostensible occupation of these unfortunates is that of the washerwoman, but large numbers are engaged in brewing Kaffir beer – which is contraband – and in adding to their means of livelihood in other questionable methods. The lucrative nature of their employment has been evidenced at this office when they have had occasion to deposit money for safe custody. Individual remittances of £96 and £45 were made by women of the class mentioned.'

Marwick condemned the School Plaats Location in Pretoria and the Native Married Men's Settlement in Johannesburg. 'It is a "den of iniquity", it being a dumping ground for native burglars, a haven for native women of easy virtue and an idling place for native loafers that abound along the reef. It is an institution of the "Xhosa" native, but the number of Zulus who have so far departed from the national traditions with respect to living in adultery is increasing from day to day.'

As of January 1897 it was illegal to sell alcohol to black people. Marwick was as disapproving of sellers as he was of 'Natal natives, equally with those from

This photograph of a black man in a fashionable European outfit was taken in the 1890s. At the time he would have been an unusual sight on the streets of Johannesburg. Marwick, like many of his white contemporaries, was very critical of Zulu men who wore tailor-made suits, gambled and bought sweepstake tickets. *(Courtesy Johannesburg College of Education Library)*

other places, who contribute to the growth of this traffic as consumers'. 'However,' he said, 'several Zulus are engaged in the work of trapping liquor sellers, and the employment by the detectives of additional natives of proved integrity as auxiliaries would probably have good results.'

In addition, he was very aware of the way in which Zulus 'gave in to temptation' when they were exposed to the glitter of gold in Johannesburg. He compared their behaviour to the Bible story of the prodigal son. In very Victorian English he said, 'The extravagance of the native prodigal finds expression in gambling at cards, in the purchase of sweepstakes, tailor-made suits etc., and in boarding in an eating house, or eating in a gluttonous manner ... Of this class the professedly devout are lavish in their gifts to female churchgoers, and in this and their excess of zeal for a good cause ... they ultimately become unmindful of their natural obligations to the community from which they have sprung.'

Marwick felt strongly that the Zulus who worked on the Rand should be there only to earn money to pay their taxes and support their families at home. They should not be taking part in gambling, be wearing tailor-made suits, or be living like white miners in boarding-houses. They should not drink illegally brewed liquor and should not visit prostitutes or give too many gifts to 'female churchgoers' if they had families at home who depended on them.

Marwick shared many of the views generally held by white people at the time.

'One may not overlook the maxim that "individuals and communities of a very low state of intelligence are always improvident",' he said and added that one needed to be intellectually developed to be able to plan for the future. However, having voiced criticism of black people in this way, his next paragraph states that most of the Zulus who visited his office did do exactly as he would have liked all of them to do. 'Side by side with the spendthrift, but in predominating numbers, there are found natives whose entire energy is employed in providing for the satisfaction of some pressing need in Natal, and it is with these that this office has most to do.'

Marwick's 1897 report on his work on the Rand does not describe the individuals he worked with every day. Only after the war, in 1904, when he was back in Johannesburg working as a native agent, did Marwick keep a diary. In it, he described a range of people and their troubles: One can assume that he would have handled the same kind of problems from 1895 until the outbreak of the war in 1899.

Life on the gold-fields was hard, especially for married men who brought their wives with them. Old rules of behaviour no longer counted. Johanna Sililo and her husband Samuel had a fight about another man, for example, and brought their troubles to Marwick.

In his personal record Marwick noted (often ignoring strict grammatical conventions): 'Johanna Sililo explains that her husband Samuel Sililo deserted her three years ago and that he has not returned to her since. Samuel stated: "My wife's statement about the marriage certificate is true. I quarrelled with her because she handed the certificate to Solomon Mahlangana. I reported to the authorities when my wife went to Charlie Hlongwane's where Solomon was living. I was told to look for her, I went with Matios to look for her and found her in bed with Charlie Hlongwane. She asked when I would bring a case against her. I reported to the authorities and I was told to watch her at night. I went one morning at six o'clock and found her in bed with Solomon. The police told them to dress and accompany them. The authorities there gave no order about the matter. I subsequently got a letter from a law agent warning me not to molest my wife and Solomon."

'Johanna Sililo said very briefly: "The child on my back is mine. Joseph Kistens, another man, is the father. Johanna agrees to return to her husband."'

In another case Sam and Emma Ndoba fought about money. 'Emma states that she gave Sam money to buy stand licences, but he appropriated it for his own uses. The amount she gave him was £2 10s. for licenses and £1 for the purpose of buying trousers. The amount she required for stand licenses is £3 2s. 6d. Partners agree to live together again,' Marwick concluded.

Bantsi, a member of Chief Daniel Mamogale's clan, and his wife Rosina of Rietkop in Pretoria came to see Marwick because Bantsi complained that Rosina had left him three months previously. Bantsi told his story: 'Two weeks ago I came to Johannesburg to fetch my wife and found her living with another man,

Frans, in the Indian Location. We were married according to native custom about 1894. I want my wife back. We have had six children, four of whom are dead. The two surviving children are with Rosina at the Indian Location. I mentioned I have no quarrel with my wife.'

Rosina gave her side of the story: 'I have been beaten by Bantsi, that's why I left him. I cannot use my left hand properly owing to the injuries inflicted by Bantsi. When Bantsi came to Johannesburg to fetch me he reported at No. 3 Pass Office and then it was decided that he should take me to Bethanie. He agreed while at the office, but afterwards said I should go to Bethanie and he would follow in the winter. I said I would not go back unless he came at once. I do not wish to go back to Bantsi but wish him to take me back to my people (my uncle) and my chief. My parents are dead.'

Marwick noted that 'the parties agree to lay the matter before their chief at Bethanie, Rustenburg'.

Marwick was also called upon to give advice to Annie and Ezekiel Mvimbi. Annie, already an older woman said, 'I was married to Ezekiel Mvimbi at Burghersdorp about 1890 by Reverend M Hodges, the Wesleyan Minister. The marriage was solemnised in the church. Ezekiel left me in 1893 at Burghersdorp and went to Kimberley. There he was imprisoned for theft for three years. I was in Kimberley in 1895 when he was discharged. He refused to return home. I went home to Burghersdorp but as he did not come, I proceeded to Johannesburg in

1899. He found me in September 1903. We quarrelled after two months and he drove me away. I have not been back since. I claim my old wedding dress and marriage certificate and six boxes containing my goods and those of my sister and a friend.'

Ezekiel Mvimbi said, 'On 20 November 1903 I quarrelled with my wife. We swore at each other a great deal. I was on night shift and often taking my rest. I found that my wife was gone. I looked for her, but could not find her. In the middle of the night she returned with a constable and a Native policeman. She went away with the police and has not been back since.'

Marwick noted the outcome of the dispute on 11 March 1904. 'Parties refuse to live together again. They were informed of procedure in case of either wishing for a divorce and of the ground on which such could be claimed.' Unfortunately Annie made no mention of what happened to her while she was trapped in Johannesburg during the war!

Children were equally affected by their parents' disrupted life on the Rand. A man, Samson, also called Samseu, claimed custody of a nine-year-old child called Bella from her grandmother, Tiswayo. Samseu said, 'I claim custody of my child. The mother, Nomasotsha, was not married to me. I was about to *lobola* her, but she went away with Petros, alias Limana. I live in the Wakkerstroom district. I met Nomasotsha there and I had connection with her, the issue being the child Bella. My brother, Petros, alias Limana, took Nomasotsha and went

51

away with her to the Orange River Colony.'

Tiswayo said, 'I do not refuse to give up the child if the father is prepared to *lobola* the mother. Let them bring the cattle and I will fulfil my part. Nomasotsha is my daughter, her father Majulina is dead. Nomasothsa had one child to Samseu and three to Petros alias Limana; one of the last-mentioned children is dead, the other two are at Petros' kraal. Nomasotsha is in jail in Johannesburg. She is imprisoned for making Kaffir beer. She lives in the Johannesburg Location with Petros. Three cattle were fair to me, but I reckon they paid a beast (*invenda*) and subsequently took and sold it to a white man. When they bought the three head, I accepted them in place of the *invenda* that had been taken away from me. I received a horse also in place of the *invenda*.'

Marwick noted on 12 March 1904: 'The child appears to belong to the state of Mafuluka. Parties informed accordingly unless the woman Nomasotsha be *lobolaed* by Samseu or Petros.'

Besides dealing with family problems in person, the personnel at the native agent's office often wrote letters for Zulus to send home along with their money. 'In writing and reading of such, one is enabled to glean facts of interest with regard to the condition of Natives here, and of their correspondents,' Marwick added. A few replies to such letters still exist.[8]

In 1904 the wife of a man called Sibiko received £10 from Johannesburg and sent Marwick this letter of thanks.

She used the nickname which people had begun to use, Muhle, which means good or kind. She dictated the letter to the priest at the Church of Norway Mission in Natal in Zulu.

Eh Muhle, we said to the priest that we should thank you very much. We are very glad about what we reported to you. We also reported to Hlongabeza and to the court. A telephone call was made and we were told that he [Sibiko] was nowhere to be found. We were surprised to know that he had been found after we had lost hope. We would like him to come home and we request you, chief, to put him on the train because even the priest is worried about the wife who is very sick. As a woman I cannot just abandon another woman who is all by herself at home. Here at Hlongabeza's home all people think that he has deserted, because we all thought that he will solve the problems he left behind when he returns. On the month that he promised he will return home please take the money from him and send it to us if he does not return home. However, what we actually want, chief, is for our husband to come back home. I have written about four letters to him but he never replies. Chief I end here.

Sarah Ann Dlambula from Matatiele sent a similar letter in Zulu.

*To Mr Muhle
My kind Chief
Help me send Alfred Dlambula home. His mother is very ill. She fainted already three times and upon recovering on the second occasion she said that she wanted her child*

Alfred to come and bury her. I am sorry and astonished because when he left he said he was going to work for the debts he owed, but he never did send any money towards those debts.

In consequence of the said debts my two houses were sold as also my grain and bedsteads. My children are starving and I am living in the town in Matatiele.

Help me my chief Muhle and send Alfred down not only as far as the train runs but as far as I am living (Matatiele) and here please to hand him over into my hands.

May I end so far my chief.

When Alfred returned home, Sarah wrote to Marwick again.

Dear Sir,
Yes my Lord Alfred is here at home and I don't know how may I thank your kindness, deeds you had done by sending him to me ...

Nomakwa, wife of Sigqili Mhkingo from the Adams Mission Station in Natal, sent this letter to Marwick.

Sir
You will be surprised to receive a letter from a person who is unknown to you. I am a widow, my husband died about twenty-five years ago, and I have got two sons Zixibilili and July. My eldest son Zixibilili left here about fourteen years ago, I hear that he works for the solicitor in court there in Johannesburg, close to your office. And I also hear that he is pretty well known to everybody in the court by the name of William Mhlango. Your native police Salane know him very well by the name of Zixibilili

Mhlango. I will be very pleased indeed if you send him down at once by so doing I will be very pleased indeed. We are now paying £3 in the Mission Reserves every year and I don't know what to do as I have nobody to help me. Please send him at once. Before you send him down, please let him get all his things, he is always at the court there.

She added a little flattery:

Bryant Mtetwa of Imfune told me that you are a big chief there and you can help me by bringing my son down. If I ask you, he also told me that you are a very good man indeed.

Her request to Marwick soon bore fruit, because a month later, her son had arrived home safely.

Marwick even traced criminals back to Natal. He told this story: 'There came into my office a mine manager called Wilson who had been robbed of £200 by his Zulu servant on Christmas night. He sprawled into a chair, hatchet-faced and cadaverous, with beetling brows and shower-lantern jaws, and a billy-goat beard to add to his gravity. "I have been robbed, robbed by my kitchenboy. I offer £100 reward for this arrest. I'm told you're the only man who can find him.

'"On Christmas night," he said, "I had in my trousers' pockets £100 in gold, £100 in notes, a gold watch inscribed 'From a friend' and a twenty dollar gold piece! I woke at daybreak to find my trousers missing, and went to the yard to look for the kitchenboy, Jim. I found that he had gone with his kit," Wilson concluded.

'The problem of tracing an elusive Jim

The staff of the Natal Native Department. According to the inscription, J S Marwick is seated in the middle with a Mr Wallace on his left and a Mr Whielwright (probably Guy Wheelwright) on his right. The four black men, on whose uniforms the insignia of their employer are clearly visible, were not identified. (*Courtesy South African National Museum of Military History*)

among the 200,000 natives on the Witwatersrand looked a difficult one. I eventually heard that Jim was known to his friends by the name Sogwebu and that he belonged to the Mazibuko clan. I lost no time in circulating to the Natal police in the three districts in which the Mazibukos used to be found, all the information I could glean about the wanted man. Within a month I received a telegram from the Natal police, Ladysmith:

"Sogwebu alias Jim arrested".

'Jim, who had thrown the gold dollar piece into the Klipriver because he thought that it was not money, was extradited to stand trial at Boksburg. Before he could be tried he died at the Johannesburg Fort, much to the disgust of the mine manager. Mr Wilson said resignedly, "Well, I'm glad he's dead." But, with a regretful shake of the head, he concluded, "I wish I'd had the killing of him!"'

Chapter 5

THE THREAT OF WAR

Early in 1899 the people of Johannesburg, black and white, knew war was threatening to break out between the ZAR and Great Britain. In June, July and August Marwick sent the messengers from his office up and down the Reef trying to allay the fears of the Zulus about the war. He also kept his bosses in Natal informed of the growing tensions.

'On the 9th of June 1899, I reported to the Under-Secretary for Native Affairs that the tension in the Transvaal political situation was making itself felt among the Natal natives on the Witwatersrand Goldfields, a large number of such natives, having sought my advice as to the course they should adopt in view of the tendency of European inhabitants to become panic-stricken and to leave the Republic.

'In the Johannesburg office and at Germiston the officers in charge have always made a point of being approachable at all times to native applicants, and in this way it became possible for the greater number of our natives to get advice and attention at first hand. Both offices thus gained a large "following", each individual native having confidence in the officers through personal acquaintance with them.'[1]

Before June, even, white and black people were beginning to pack their belongings to leave Johannesburg, either to go to their homes in the rural areas or to take refuge in towns like Durban, Port Elizabeth and Cape Town. There they would wait and see what would happen. White people locked their houses on the Reef and many told their black servants to stay behind and look after their houses until they returned. Some employers merely left and did not even pay their servants. On 21 June 1899 *The Star* newspaper mentioned that there were hundreds of black people leaving, especially for Natal. It called this 'an exodus of Natal natives'. Others who were not leaving were preparing to do so at a moment's notice. Marwick reported: 'Natal natives, more than any of their coloured brethren from elsewhere, realise the necessity for keeping by them an amount sufficient not only for ordinary expenses, but to meet any unforeseen demand.'

By early October the situation in Johannesburg had worsened considerably for the black population. The *Standard and Diggers' News* reported several incidents in which black miners started riots. In one instance, on

During the uncertain weeks leading up to the war huge crowds of people gathered at various places in Johannesburg, in an effort to find out what was happening. Here a crowd had assembled on Market Square in the centre of town. *(Courtesy Killie Campbell Africana Library)*

3 October in Boksburg, more than a thousand miners looted stores and rooms at the East Rand Mines and attacked a storekeeper when he refused to give the rioters free alcohol. The local police were powerless to interfere and stopped the riot only with the help of the Boksburg commando. The men in the commando had been loading their kit onto a train at the station to leave for the Natal frontier when the Field Cornet ordered them to gallop to the mines to quell the disorder.

As the mines closed down and the white miners left for the coast, black miners were abandoned without work or food. Government officials debated whether to commandeer trains from the NZASM to return miners, mostly from Portuguese East Africa, to the border town of Ressano Garcia. In the meantime, a company, Johannesburg Consolidated Gold Fields, reported that 'a large number of natives are at large, and threaten to attack the mine, property and loot stores.' At the Ferreira mine, too, there was what was called a 'miniature disturbance', which, it was thought, was caused by she-beens that 'had maddened the natives with drink, and it required a strong patrol of police to check the uproar'.

A number of mounted police under one Lieutenant Oosthuizen escorted a large group of miners from Roodepoort, a mining village on the West Rand, to Orange Grove on the eastern outskirts of Johannesburg, close to the road which led towards the coast and Delagoa Bay. They warned the miners, 'Return to your homes otherwise the burghers will shoot you like dogs if you attempt any further act of aggression or disturbance of the peace.' To prevent further riots large groups of ZAR policemen, about 400 men on horses, patrolled the Rand.

One such patrol overpowered a number of men who began rioting in the Native Location in the centre of Johannesburg. Burghers in nearby Vrededorp and Fordsburg 'came out fully armed and drove the natives in; and subsequently the white police, aided by native armed police got them well under control.'

One journalist who reported on this riot tried to understand why the black men had begun to riot. 'These natives are not boys from the mines, and have nothing to do with Mr Durr's scavenging boys, but are loafers, swelled by the numerous boys out of work through their employers going away. Doubtless these natives are feeling the pinch very severely. Their trade has left them, they cannot get food and lack of means prevents their getting away; hence they break bounds.'[2]

Katie Makanya, a young married domestic servant at the time, remembered what it was like in Johannesburg just before the outbreak of the war:

The Jeppe commando, fully armed, posed to have their photograph taken just before the outbreak of the war. Commandos such as this one had been used on numerous occasions to bring riots on the gold-fields under control or to disperse gatherings. *(Courtesy Rare Book Collection, Rand Afrikaans University: Library Services)*

'Marwick came and told all the people that we must go home because of the war, because the Boers would treat us very badly. Some of the Boers were very cruel. They even came into our church to listen and find out what we prayed. And after the war we went back and found our homes looted and the crockery broken. But we were not afraid of the English at that time.

'So Mr Marwick told the men they must all go, but they must send the women and children first. But my husband did not want to come because he had a store in the Germiston Location and he made harnesses and mended saddles and things like that. But Mr Marwick kept coming all the time and when the women had left, and I had already come to Durban, he still went and told the men, "Now you must go because this train today may be the last train." But my husband did not want to go until one day the Boers came into his store. And he had a saddle there he had mended for a white man and he was just waiting for the white man to come and fetch it. And the Boers took that saddle and also another one, and the harnesses, and they took even the soap to wash the leather. So the next day my husband went to the white man and said the Boers had taken the saddle. And the white man was not

Scores of people, both black and white, desperately tried to flee Johannesburg in order to avoid being trapped there for the duration of the war. In this photograph black men, women and children wait at Park station for the arrival of a train to take them home. The fashionably dressed black woman on the right continued walking as the photograph was taken. On the left two sewing machines can be seen amongst the luggage. (*Courtesy South African National Museum of Military History*)

angry. He said, "I know how it is. They took my horses yesterday." And the Boers took all those things from my husband and did not pay him one penny. And so the next time Mr Marwick came, my husband said he would catch the train. And then the train he caught was indeed the last one.'[3]

About one thousand black people were still trying to leave, as they always did, by applying for travelling permits from the Pass Office. They were mainly miners who had been dismissed by the mines without notice. Government officials at this office had to try to find ways of getting these workers back home. Still nothing had been done to find trains to transport them. People waited for the Field Cornet of Johannesburg and the Mining Commissioner to come to some kind of decision.

Marwick telegraphed to his head office in Natal for guidance. 'The Zulus should be told to buy a train ticket or to stay in Johannesburg where I will try to see to their welfare,' he said. The Natal government sent him £300 for expenses and ordered him to remain in Johannesburg. But towards the end of September things changed rapidly. Thousands of British and other foreigners closed their businesses and many of the mines, and left their workers to fend for themselves.

Marwick's office was inundated by Zulus who wanted to return to their homes. Marwick had heard rumours too that the Natal Railway Agency, which operated the railway in Natal, was closing down and did not know what would happen to their offices, both in Johannesburg and Germiston. 'I would

be of more use to the Zulus staying in Johannesburg. I promised the Zulus to give them warning at the earliest possible moment and to assist them to get out of the country. If their earnings could be remitted to Natal through our agency, they would be safeguarded from robbery en route,' he told his superiors in Natal.

In the meantime, Marwick went to Pretoria to ask the ZAR government for protection for the Natal natives in general. Although he was given an interview by the State Secretary F W Reitz, the Minister of Mines B J Kleinhans and Commandant-General P J Joubert in Pretoria, Marwick returned to Johannesburg without promises of protection or help.

By the end of September 1899 everyone on the Rand knew that war was imminent. From 27 September Boer commandos were being sent to the Natal border on trains which the ZAR government had taken over from the NZASM.

On 29 September Marwick again went to Pretoria. 'What should I do?' he asked Conyngham Greene, the British Agent.

'Our Natal natives should leave the Transvaal as soon as possible,' the Agent replied. 'How do you propose to assist their departure?'

'There is a difficulty in connection with the Pass Law. An employer who withholds permission for natives to leave his service could deny them the right to obtain passes enabling them to travel to their homes,' Marwick replied.

'I have a large stock of railway tickets bearing the endorsement "Natal Agent",' Marwick continued. 'If the authorities at Pretoria would agree to regard such tickets

The newly built Raadzaal on Church Square, Pretoria – the seat of government of the ZAR. It housed the offices of the president and other high-ranking officials. After the discovery of gold, the ZAR's new-found wealth enabled the government to erect a number of imposing government buildings. The Raadzaal was designed by the Dutch architect Sytze Wierda and was completed in 1892. *(Courtesy Transnet Heritage Library)*

as a sufficient pass for any native returning home, the difficulty would be overcome. The authorities should simply instruct their officials in this regard.'

'Agreed,' replied the Agent. 'Go ahead.'

Marwick went immediately to see the State Secretary, Reitz, but he was unwilling to grant Marwick's request. From his office Marwick went directly to the Commandant-General's office. General Joubert kindly agreed to his proposal and telegraphed the border officials to give them the necessary instructions.

'On my return to Johannesburg, natives were informed of the arrangement and about one thousand men took advantage of the opportunity on the 1st of October,' Marwick concluded.

But on 2 October passenger traffic to Natal was suspended. Rather than sending them back to the railway offices, Marwick's office refunded the men their tickets and collected the money from the railways themselves. The NZASM halted all passenger train services between the Rand and Natal. All trains were to be used by the Boer army in preparation for the coming war.

Marwick had to put his back-up plan into action. 'It became necessary for me to arrange other means of removing our natives who congregated at the office in their thousands. The Germiston office was closed and Mr Wheelwright, the officer in charge, came to assist me in Johannesburg. On the 2nd of October I went to Pretoria. I called at the Commandant-General's office to ask that I should be allowed to take all Natal natives home by road.'

But General Joubert had already left by train for Sandspruit, close to the Natal border, where the Boer army was mustering to prepare for the invasion of Natal. His secretary, Mr Louis de Souza, was aghast at this request. He said, 'You will be leading the natives into certain death, as the Transvaal commandos would be sure to fire on such a large party advancing towards their lines.'

Nevertheless De Souza went to speak to President Paul Kruger himself. 'He decided that it would still be better for the Zulus to wait in Johannesburg until they could be sent home by train. The president promised to instruct the NZASM to prepare for a large amount of native passenger traffic to the Natal border,' De Souza told Marwick. 'Although the line is at present blocked with commando trains, the natives should be sent as soon as a train could be run for them. It would probably be at four o'clock on the 3rd of October 1899, the President had promised.'

Not entirely trusting this promise, Marwick also telegraphed General Joubert, who had reached Heidelberg station, about his plan to take the natives home by road. 'I have no objection to the plan,' Joubert telegraphed in reply.

When 3 October dawned, no trains had arrived. Marwick telegraphed State Secretary Reitz and Commandant-General Joubert. 'When would trains be available for natives? I should be allowed to go by road with the natives, if no trains are available.' On 4 October, even though the directors of the NZASM gave permission for the use of their trains, the local rail traffic manager at Elandsfontein, the railway yard near Germiston, gave Marwick a written statement: 'We will not be able to organise the necessary transport for the natives.'

Marwick telegraphed the news to De Souza. The ZAR government replied, 'The Transvaal government cannot say when trains would be available for natives. Zulus would be permitted to travel home by road. But there should not be more than fifty men in each gang; one European in charge of every gang.'

Louis de Souza sent Marwick the following telegram: 'In compliance with your request, I herewith enclose a Pass or Certificate of leave for yourself and about 5,000 Natal Zulu Natives from Johannesburg to the Natal Border as well as a copy of a telegram to Commandant van Dam to send six policemen to accompany the natives, the reasonable expense thereof calculated at about one pound per man per day, to be borne by you. I further enclose a copy of a telegram to Commandant-General Joubert now at Sandspruit informing him of the departure of the natives. This permission and pass are granted to you on the strict understanding that you hold yourself responsible for the peaceful and orderly conduct of the natives while on their way and for their travelling direct and unarmed to the Natal Border.'[4]

Marwick rushed to Pretoria. At last he had the permission he needed, even though the conditions attached would be very difficult to meet. He saw De Souza at his home at nine o'clock that night. 'I then received safe-conduct papers to enable me to take the natives home in one large body by road. I could then be in Johannesburg on the morning of the 5th to complete arrangements for our journey to Natal,' Marwick concluded. In the days before fast trains and cars, Marwick indeed completed these journeys between Johannesburg and Pretoria in record time, most probably on horseback.

De Souza also organised the escort of the Transvaal Mounted Police for Marwick's journey. 'I ordered Commandant van Dam of Johannesburg to supply six policemen for the journey. You will have to pay Van Dam one pound per man per day for ten days, the length of time you calculated that the journey would last,' he told Marwick.

Marwick still had to deal with his own bosses in Natal. They were not very supportive of his plans. On 5 October 1899 Marwick sent three telegrams to the Under-Secretary for Native Affairs, O S Samuelson, in Pietermaritzburg explaining these developments. In the first telegram he warned, 'There is no work here for natives, and authorities wish them to go. If the natives do not leave, the police will have to clear them out of town, and they may starve on the veldt. I am perfectly willing to remain at post, but foresee that the only way to save the lives and earnings of natives here is to take them home ... I am not acting hastily, and have been advised on all hands to get natives away ... If I sit still and wait on railway people, though they also advise the road journey, five thousand natives already unemployed will be stranded, and I shall be regarded as having cut them adrift; if I do otherwise, I am also discredited and dismissed. I await telegram this afternoon.' He firmly believed that he would be able to help the Zulus to return home.

In the second telegram of the day, in a heroic gesture, Marwick tried to force a reply by offering to resign. 'So that my proposed action may not embarrass you, please suspend me from office. If I get natives through without loss of life, you could please yourself about reinstating me; if not, I would not expect reinstatement.'

At last he received a reply from the Under-Secretary for Native Affairs. Reluctantly he gave Marwick permission but warned him not to spend too much money. 'Provided you have official documents from the Transvaal Government, giving you safe conduct for yourself and the natives, and provided also that you have an escort given to you of the six Transvaal police, as stated in your telegram, you are authorised to come out with the natives and get back to Natal at once. You must be careful that only Zululand and Natal natives accompany you ... You should organise them under *induna*ships otherwise you may have natives from other parts following you into Natal. If natives other than Natal and Zululand natives attempt to follow you, you should seek the assistance of the Transvaal authorities to turn them back. Wheelwright is given discretion to leave his post. Transfer your account to Pietermaritzburg.'

Another telegram from the Natal Prime Minister followed: 'Incur such expenditure as you may consider necessary for the purpose, keeping a careful account of the amount expended and exercising due economy.'

Neither the Under-Secretary nor the Prime Minister thought it necessary to wish Marwick good luck on the journey he was about to undertake.

On 6 October, just before leaving

Representing
Natal &
Zululand
Native
Affairs.

Johannesburg, Marwick sent two more telegrams: 'Telegrams of yesterday and today received. Safe-conduct papers from Commandant-General have been handed to me and escort told off. We leave daylight tomorrow; expect to reach Volksrust within six days ...' The second telegram reads: 'Honourable Prime Minister's telegram received, and account shall be kept accordingly. We have to pay £60 for escort; do not anticipate other expenditure.'[5]

At the same time a Zulu, Hlobeni Buthelezi, came to Marwick. ''Nkosi, you have sent home your staff for their own safety. Allow me to be your Head Marshall and to collect suitable men to keep order, during our long march. My ancestor Masingula Buthelezi was the Prince Minister of King Mpande, and I am well known to all the Zulus.' Marwick accepted his offer. Cloth armbands were ordered for all the men who were given the job to maintain order on the march.

The morning before the march, when Marwick still had to deal with a number of problems, a lark flew over their heads.

''Nkosi,' said Buthelezi, 'that is a happy omen. That bird's song means that good fortune will be ours. No one ever hears such a greeting without being confident that his day will be a joyous one.'[6]

This fragment of a photograph of the men who represented the Natal and Zululand Native Affairs Department on the Reef, shows Marwick, seated, with an unnamed assistant standing behind him. *(Courtesy Killie Campbell Africana Library)*

Chapter 6

THE LONG MARCH HOME

The march was on. 'Go up and down the reef and tell the Zulus about this chance to get away from Johannesburg. Tell the men to bring with them enough food to last for five days and tell them to come and bank their money with officials at the offices in Marshall Street in Johannesburg,' Marwick instructed the messengers.[1]

Katie Makanya remembered what happened to her husband's friend, Mbombu: 'At the time of the war, he worked in the kitchen of a house, and his mistress asked him to stay and look after the place while she and her husband ran away to Cape Town. So he did not obey when Mr Marwick came to the house and told Mbombu that he would soon be in very bad trouble if he did not go.

'And now there were no more trains at all. And there were still many men in Johannesburg, and now that the war had come and there were no more trains, many of them believed Mr Marwick when he told them they must go. And so they said they would go. And that last group who came, they had to walk from Johannesburg all the way to Charlestown on the Natal border. Mbombu told me they had to walk and they had nothing to eat. They had money but they could not buy anything because the Boers had gone through and taken everything from the stores and the fields, and sometimes it rained, and so they pulled their belts tighter. And Mr Marwick walked with them all that way. He did not ride a horse, but he walked with them himself, and he did not have anything to eat. The people think a lot of Mr Marwick. He was a real man, that one.'[2]

But before the march began, a great deal of work had to be done at the Natal Native Agent's office in Marshall Street.

'While I was engaged in negotiations with the Commandant-General's office in Pretoria, my colleague, Wheelwright, rendered splendid service at the office in Johannesburg. From early morning till late at night he was busily engaged with natives who were desirous of sending their moneys to Natal. Throughout a period of intense excitement he showed himself to be cool and resourceful in the management of the natives. Thousands surrounded the office buildings. From time to time, while I was absent, Mr Wheelwright had to go up to the balcony and address the vast crowd. He was always able to command orderly

A crowd of black men assembled in the street, possibly Marshall Street, in front of the offices of the Natal Native Agency in Johannesburg, waiting for news about the impending war. They were all wearing hats according to the fashion of the time. *(Courtesy Killie Campbell Africana Library)*

behaviour.' During the three days before the march, the men sent nearly £10 000 to Natal in the form of workers' wages.

Although Marwick and Wheelwright were working very hard, they could not keep up with the demands of the crowd outside their office. The part of Marshall Street where their office was situated was completely blocked by workers. On the evening of 5 October, the police persuaded the workers to go to the Witwatersrand Agricultural Showgrounds for the night, while waiting for the march to begin.

FRIDAY 6 OCTOBER 1899

On the morning of Friday 6 October Mr E Holgate of the New Heriot mine came to them. 'I have brought you, free of charge, a Cape cart and a pair of horses as well as a four-wheeled trap and a pair of horses which belong to the company. Use it on your journey. May I introduce Mr W A Connorton, also from the company. He would like to join you on the journey as your secretary. He also brought along a Cape cart and a pair of horses.' Wheelwright and Connorton decided to travel on the cart. Marwick found a pony for himself.

The forthcoming march was big news. It was even bigger news because other native agents had used the tension and confusion of the previous few days once again to defraud black miners. A reporter of *The Star* picked up this story. 'Some two hundred East Coast boys who had been working on some of the mines out Krugersdorp way, arrived at Park Station last night [by train]. The unfortunate men were under the impression that they were going to Komatie Poort, but were bundled out at Park Station. From what could be understood from these natives it would appear that they had given an agent money for their tickets to Komatie Poort as well as a bonus of 2/6 per head for his trouble, and that he had simply got them tickets to Park Station.'[3]

A *Standard and Diggers' News* report highlighted the way in which Marwick, in contrast, was organising his march. 'An immense crowd of natives assembled yesterday morning outside the Natal Native Agency near Marshall Square. They had been marched from the Agricultural Society Showground where they had spent the previous night. Mr J S Marwick, the Natal Native Agent, made a speech to them in Zulu. "The Government has given permission for you to march to the Natal border under the escort of six mounted police. Those of you who have not already sent your money home, do so through the banks. Otherwise you may be robbed or attacked on the road," Marwick warned. A large number of these natives left the previous night, and were to encamp at Klipriver on the Natal Road. The remainder of the 5 000 leave today,' the report concluded.[4]

The 'gang', as Marwick called the marchers, was on the move. At last 'the Honourable Secretary for Native Affairs signified approval of the arrangements for bringing the natives home'. Marwick sighed with relief. He had not been fired, as he thought he could have been.

'Departing today. Please inform land-drosts en route so that provision merchants will know we are coming. Telegraph General Joubert at Sandspruit. Advise the commandos that we have set out,' he telegraphed De Souza.

Mr Holgate of the New Heriot mine donated a Cape cart like the one in the picture to Marwick. The cart and two horses, which Holgate also donated, were used on the march. This picture was taken in 1894, in front of one of the newly-built railway houses in Heidelberg, the first town on the marchers' route. *(Courtesy Transnet Heritage Library)*

Above: Map showing the route from Johannesburg to Heidelberg. (*Courtesy Map Collection, University of the Witwatersrand Library*)

At Sandspruit, however, General Joubert himself had other problems to solve. Already on 4 October he had telegraphed Pretoria: 'Trains lie blocked, people cannot get here, are hungry, have no food or horse fodder.'[5]

A large Boer armed force was gathering at Sandspruit, some 16 kilometres from the Natal border. Seventeen-year-old Deneys Reitz, son of former President of the Orange Free State, F W Reitz, arrived at Sandspruit with the Pretoria Commando. In his journal he recorded: 'There were great numbers of burghers from the country districts already encamped on the plain, on either side of the railway line, and the veld on all sides was dotted with tents and wagon-laagers. On the left of the track stood a large marquee over which floated the Vierkleur flag of the Transvaal, indicating General Joubert's headquarters. Both he and his wife were thus early on the scene, it being her invariable custom to accompany her husband in the field.'

In Johannesburg Marwick escorted the first group of workers out of town. Later he recalled: 'At 5 p.m. I marched out as far as Klipriviersberg (seven miles) on the Natal Road, with about four thousand

67

natives and left them with Corporal Nel and four troopers of the Transvaal Mounted Police. I told the workers, "I promise to rejoin you at daylight tomorrow. I will bring the remainder of the natives. But first I must return to Johannesburg."'

SATURDAY 7 OCTOBER 1899

On 7 October, at five o'clock in the morning, Marwick again set out from Johannesburg. 'Corporal Williams and Troopers Van Seil, Veuren, Putter Bretz and Miles, of the Transvaal Mounted Police, reported themselves at the office. Corporal Williams had been placed in charge of our escort by my special request. We proceeded, together with a large number of natives, to Klipriviersberg. I paid off Corporal Nel and his men at 5s. each for the night duty. Corporal Williams placed himself under my orders. I found him extremely obliging, and an excellent officer.

'When I reached Klipriviersberg a crowd of about 7,000 natives must have been there. It was wonderful to see the eagerness with which they set out on their long tramp. The first morning was remarkable for the frequency of the greeting one heard from the natives. On every hand we doubted as to how the journey would end. Yet I could not but feel that the large horde had confidence in my ability to lead them through.'

The Zulus proclaimed, 'Child of the Englishman, but for whose presence none might brave the Boers.'

They saluted Marwick: 'Care for the dark race.'

And saluted him again: 'Gather the orphans of the Zulu.'

These tributes gave Marwick courage for the undertaking. They convinced him that the men would be amenable to the strict discipline that would be necessary on the march.

The first leg of the march to Heidelberg could begin. 'Take two mounted policemen and ride about three miles in advance of the gang. Inform the people on the roadside of our approach,' Marwick ordered Corporal Williams.

The group left Klipriviersberg and travelled to Klip Spruit, about 24 kilometres from Johannesburg. Here they rested for two hours. A man who owned a shop in the neighbourhood sold all the foodstuff he had to the men. He then proceeded to cheat them by selling caustic soda which is used for making soap and can cause great damage if swallowed and soft soap in tins, under the misrepresentation that the tins contained corned beef or jam.

'Stop this,' Marwick ordered the police, 'and also stop the sale of liquor to the natives.'

The local Field Cornet, Van der Westhuizen, visited the marchers. He warned Marwick, 'The arrival of the natives has caused great alarm among my neighbours. Be careful.'

After midday the group left Klip Spruit and walked to Rietvlei. Here they stopped to wait for Wheelwright and Connorton who had remained in Johannesburg to close all the bank accounts. When the two men caught up with them, the crowd moved on to Heidelberg. They met a Boer

Top: The newly-constructed station at Rietvlei, a small siding between Johannesburg and Heidelberg. On this treeless grassland the marchers waited for Wheelwright and Connorton to arrive from Johannesburg, where they closed all the bank accounts of the Natal Native Agency before departing. *(Courtesy Transnet Heritage Library)*
Bottom: One of the many rocky kloofs in the Suikerbosrand near Heidelberg where the marchers could find shelter. The men preferred the kloof to the campsite at the Heidelberg water reservoir which was exposed to the piercing highveld wind. *(Courtesy Transnet Heritage Library)*

patrol some eight kilometres from the town. What happened between the patrol and the marchers is not recorded.

On that first day, they made good progress. Marwick recalled, 'The gang arrived at Heidelberg just after dark at 7.30 p.m. We found a camping ground for the night close to the water reservoir of the town. Soon it became so cold that large numbers of natives moved during the night into the rocky hills above the town. Here they found nooks that were sheltered from the wind.'

SUNDAY 8 OCTOBER 1899

Looking down from the rocky outcrops on the slopes of the Suikerbosrand, where the marchers had spent the night, they saw the town below them. Heidelberg was a pretty town of about 3 000 people, situated in the quiet countryside, far removed from the dust and din of the Rand mining towns. It

With its white houses standing on a green slope at the foot of the Suikerbosrand, Heidelberg was considered to be a charming town in the 1890s. The marchers spent their first night away from Johannesburg in the hills in the background. *(Courtesy Transnet Heritage Library)*

was a rather important town in the ZAR. Once, during the 1880s, it had even been the capital of the republic.

The 1903 travel-guide writer, Francis Harrison, drew a contemporary picture of Heidelberg:

'The steeple of its ornate church may be seen for many miles around. The town is very pleasant in spring or summer being "bosomed high in tufted trees".'

Here the Heidelberg Commando was preparing to leave for the front.

Marwick left the marchers at the reservoir and rode into the town to look for the landdrost, Mr Wepener. His preparations and telegram to Louis de Souza had paid off. The local shopkeepers were ready to sell food and other provisions to the Zulus early on Sunday morning. The shopkeepers went out to the marchers to

The inside of the store of Mr J Reichenberg in Heidelberg, possibly one of the shopkeepers who traded with the marchers. *(Courtesy Transnet Heritage Library)*

do business. In the meantime, Marwick took his safe-conduct papers to the Heidelberg landdrost.

At Heidelberg station Marwick found out that there was still some space on trains heading for Natal. Those marchers who were ill and could not continue with

ridges which gave the landscape a broken appearance. Low brushwood was interspersed with grassland. 'At intervals there are big, for the most part round or oval-shaped, hills of basalt and sandstone, and these are very similar in appearance to the hills near Johannes-

Heidelberg station was built in the mid-1890s when the rail link between Natal and Johannesburg was constructed by the NZASM. Here about 120 members of Marwick's 'gang' were put onto one of the last trains to leave for the Natal border. *(Courtesy Transnet Heritage Foundation)*

the march would be able to get onto the overcrowded trains. Some seventy men and fifty women and children were left at the station to catch the train.

'One of them was a small Zulu girl who was suffering from fever. She had travelled in our trap from Johannesburg to Heidelberg,' Marwick recalled.

On the other side of Heidelberg, the main group turned and left the main road for a smaller road. As it had the day before, the road wound past numerous

burg, although the Heidelberg hills – some of which might almost be termed mountains – are more rugged,' Francis Harrison continued his description.

At midday the marchers halted for two hours' rest. Boers in the neighbourhood brought mealies and fowl for sale. The men bought all they could get.

At this resting place, Marwick dealt fast and harshly with the first signs of trouble. 'Two natives were behaving insolently. A case of theft was also brought to

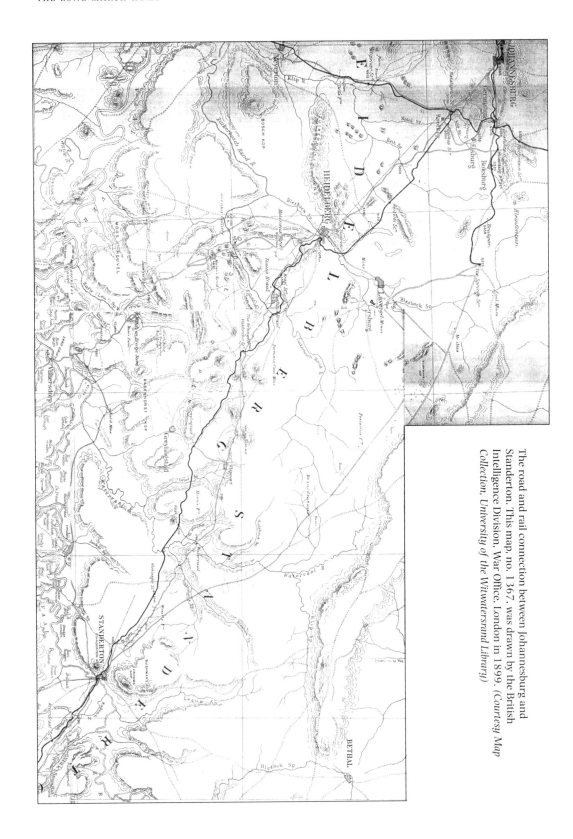

The road and rail connection between Johannesburg and Standerton. This map, no. 1367, was drawn by the British Intelligence Division, War Office, London in 1899. (*Courtesy Map Collection, University of the Witwatersrand Library*)

light. But the punishment meted out to the offenders seemed to have a salutary effect.' It would seem that even though Marwick had tried to allow only hard-working, honest men on the march, several of Johannesburg's criminals had also wormed their way into the crowd.

Ironically, Marwick also had trouble with the police escort. 'There was some unpleasantness between Corporal Williams and Veuren and Van Seil. Trooper Miles was drunk and incapable.'

In addition, according to the strict instructions Marwick had received from his bosses just before he left, he turned back all the people in the group who were not Zulus. Even before they had reached Heidelberg, he had already turned back a large group of Basuto men and 'Cape Colony natives'. On Sunday he also turned back two groups of 'Shangana' natives who were from the Mozambique province.

'At the resting place we took over a trolley owned by one of the natives in the gang for the sick. Then it became possible to carry about twelve sick men and women who might otherwise have been left behind,' Marwick recalled.

After the midday rest, the group set out again.

Marwick rode with the people at the end of the long line of marchers. 'When I came along with the rear-portion of the gang, I heard that during the afternoon a native had been seized with a sudden illness. He rode my pony until we arrived at the camping ground. Unfortunately the animal was startled by some passing natives. Although I was holding the rein the sick man was thrown and sustained a considerable shock. He was placed on the trolley when we resumed our journey.'

That day the marchers walked 56 kilometres. They made camp only when they found water at a small spruit which meandered across the increasingly flat landscape. At a brisk walking speed of five kilometres per hour, the marchers most probably had walked for more than eleven hours that day, possibly for two stretches lasting more than five hours at a time.

MONDAY 9 OCTOBER 1899

Marwick had wanted to get started early in the morning, but he experienced trouble. 'We had contemplated a very early start, but three police horses were missing. We had to wait until they were found and only at eight o'clock we proceeded. After having travelled about 15 miles, we halted for water and food. Boers brought produce for sale and the natives bought mealies and eggs from them.'

At this halt, probably in an effort to make the marchers forget the 'unpleasantness' of the previous day, the policemen demonstrated how well they could shoot. 'The native bystanders were much impressed at the unerring aim of Trooper Bretz. When Mr Wheelwright borrowed one of the police carbines and hit the same mark at first shot, their delight knew no bounds,' Marwick remarked.

'During the morning trek a native who had suffered the amputation of his toe, was lagging behind his friends, so I led the pony while he rode. A native sickening with pneumonia rode the pony from

73

WATERFALL: 6·12·94·

The marchers needed to cross several small rivers, such as the Waterfall River, which meandered across an increasingly flat landscape. This photograph, dated 6 December 1894, was probably taken by a NZASM railway engineer documenting the progress of the construction of the railway line. *(Courtesy Transnet Heritage Foundation)*

our midday resting place to the homestead of Mr Horn where we slept that night. I remained with the rear portion of the gang, to see that no footsore natives were left behind.'

On the third day and not even half-way, Marwick described how many marchers in the group were suffering: 'While all was gay in front – natives marching thirty abreast with concertinas playing the most popular native tunes – there was very great suffering among the stragglers, some of them limping along miles behind the main body, it being impossible for them to reach the sleeping place until long after the others had cooked their food and retired for the night.'

TUESDAY 10 OCTOBER 1899

On Tuesday morning the dreary march across the treeless plain to Waterfall began.

Before their departure, Mr Horn sold some ten muids (about 900 kilograms) of mealies to the marchers in small lots. On the way some marchers stole a few fowl off a cart laden with eggs and poultry, which had been abandoned alongside the road. Even before the march reached the midday halt at Bushman's Spruit, the thieves were caught and punished by Marwick's black constables in keeping with his policy of keeping a tight control on the march.

Otherwise things were going well. The store at Bushman's Spruit and farmers in the area did excellent business that day. The arrival of at least seven thousand potential customers, who allegedly had money on them, was a most unusual happening on the platteland. 'The marchers were able to obtain mealie meal, sugar, corned beef, jam and golden syrup. They quickly bought up the entire stock of such things at the store,' Marwick recorded.

'When we halted at Bushman's Spruit, a farmer arrived. "I followed you to your resting place. I have fifteen bags of mealies and some tobacco for sale as well," he said.

'Then Field Cornet Boshoff and ten men also came to see our gang. "What about meeting on the road during the afternoon?" they suggested. "We will have mutton for sale to the natives."'

At Bushman's Spruit the march encountered some trouble. Marwick continued, 'A native set fire to the veld. Immediately we called up a large number of men to put it out. A native constable traced the culprit and I had him punished. I wanted to impress on the other natives to exercise greater care with their fires.'

More members of the group had trouble keeping up with the march. Some turned to Marwick for help. 'On the 10th I travelled with the stragglers,' Marwick said, 'and a sick native was riding my pony.' Marwick hoped that they would find some help at Standerton. 'Tell the people who are unable to travel further on foot that they may be able to catch the train at Standerton,' Marwick told the constables.

At the turn of the century Standerton was a small market town of about a thousand inhabitants. It was generally considered to be 'far from attractive in appearance'. *(Courtesy Transnet Heritage Library)*

The 'gang' did not reach their resting place that night. Standerton, their destination, was a market town, even smaller than Heidelberg, with only about 1 100 black and white inhabitants. 'It was far from attractive in appearance, there being no natural features of any importance, if we except the Vaal River,' noted the traveller, Francis Harrison, a few years later.

'We slept within six miles of Standerton. The next morning we were delayed again. Three of the police horses were missing,' Marwick lamented.

At Sandspruit, between Standerton and Volksrust, more and more Boer commandos were gathering. Records show that there were 8 369 men, 5 381 horses, 398 wagons, 1 909 oxen and 1 525 tons of stores assembled on the bleak plain.[6]

Many years later Deneys Reitz recalled the celebrations of 10 October, the birthday of President Kruger, at Sandspruit. 'We mustered what was then probably the largest body of mounted men ever seen in South Africa. It was magnificent to see commando after commando file past the Commandant-General, each man brandishing hat or rifle according to his individual idea of a military salute. After the march-past we formed in mass, and galloped cheering up the slope, where Piet Joubert sat on his horse beneath an embroidered umbrella. When we came to a halt he addressed us from the saddle. I was jammed among the horsemen, so could not get close enough to hear what he was saying, but soon word was passed that an ultimatum (written and signed by my father) had been sent to the British, giving them twenty-four hours in which to withdraw their troops from the borders of the Republic, failing which there was to be war. The excitement that followed was immense. The great throng stood in its stirrups and shouted itself hoarse, and it was not until long after the Commandant-General and his retinue had fought their way through the crowd that the commandos began to disperse. The jubilation continued far into the night, and as we sat around our fires discussing the coming struggle, we heard singing and shouting from the neighbouring camps until cock-crow.'

Before they arrived at Sandspruit some of these commandos had been used to quell riots of black men on the Rand. What would happen when seven thousand unarmed Zulus came face to face with this army?

WEDNESDAY 11 OCTOBER 1899
On Wednesday morning, close to Standerton, Marwick said to Corporal Williams, 'We need to go into town. Accompany Messrs Wheelwright and Connorton in the Cape cart. We must inform the authorities of the approach of our gang.'

Marwick's preparations for the arrival of the men in Standerton were very successful. Arrangements on a large scale were made for rationing the marchers. The railway authorities agreed to carry 150 sick men to the border. Ten men who were unable to pay the railway fare were allowed to travel free of charge.

In Standerton Marwick went to the

Top: Men gathered outside one of the general dealers in Standerton. The store-owner probably took advantage of the rare opportunity to trade with 7 000 people on the march, who were hungry and tired as they arrived in town. *(Courtesy Transnet Heritage Library)*

Bottom: Standerton station was built in the same style as Heidelberg station during the construction of the NZASM railway line between Johannesburg and Volksrust. Here 150 sick marchers were able to board a train to Natal. Those who were unable to pay the fare were allowed to travel free of charge. *(Courtesy Transnet Heritage Library)*

landdrost and asked, 'Two ponies belonging to a native of our party were lost at the last sleeping place. I have sent back a small boy to look for them. Would you be so good as to inform me should they be found?'

The landdrost just laughed. 'It's rather late in the day to speak about restoring lost property,' he observed.

'Has the situation then changed since our departure from Johannesburg?'

'The last Transvaal dispatch was the ultimatum. War has been declared. Time would be up at five o'clock this afternoon,' the landdrost replied.

What Marwick had feared most had come to pass. War had been declared. The marchers were gaining on the Boer commandos stationed at Sandspruit. Would they let the gang through unharmed? Marwick had to get the Zulus to the Natal border as quickly as possible.

'The natives set out at two o'clock. It was five before I rode out of Standerton. I overtook stragglers about six miles out.' Commencing with them, Marwick informed the marchers all along the line of the serious state of affairs: 'It will be necessary to travel till past midnight tonight. When we cross Katbosch Spruit we will travel until seven o'clock and then halt for two hours. Afterwards we will set off again.'

It was a rough night for Marwick. 'Mr Connorton and I remained with a sick native who rode the pony. We missed the way and became detached from the main body until after midnight. We found the gang where they were sleeping within three miles of Paardekop,' he recorded.

Deneys Reitz also recorded what happened at Sandspruit on 11 October: 'Next day England accepted the challenge and the war began. Once more the excitement was unbounded. Fiery speeches were made, and General Joubert was received with tumultuous cheering as he rode through to address the men. Orders were issued for all commandos to be in readiness, and five days' rations of biltong and meal were issued. Flying columns were to invade Natal, and all transport was to be left behind.

'At dawn on the morning of the 12th, the assembled commandos moved off and we started our first march. As far as the eye could see the plain was alive with horsemen, guns and cattle all steadily going forward to the frontier. The scene was a stirring one, and I shall never forget riding to war with that great host.'

THURSDAY 12 OCTOBER 1899

Reitz recorded the events of 12 October. 'We reached the border village of Volksrust before noon, and here the entire force was halted for the day, the Pretoria men camping beside the monument erected to commemorate the Battle of Majuba, fought on the mountain nearby in 1881.' The Battle of Majuba was the decisive clash between the Boers and the British during the war of 1881. The British force was annihilated – some 280 British soldiers were killed, wounded or captured by the Boers. With the defeat of the British eighteen years earlier, the independence of the ZAR was guaranteed.

Outside Standerton, early that same morning, Marwick ordered the bull

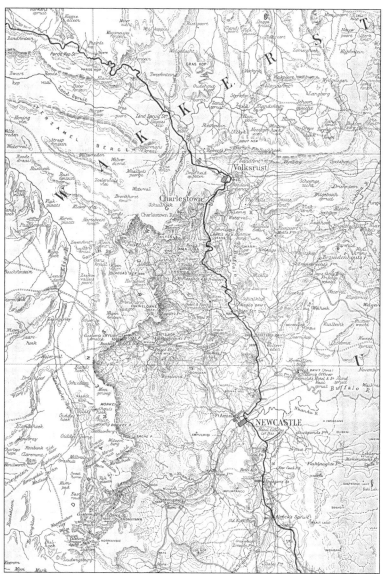

This map, no. 1367, drawn by the British Intelligence Division, London War Office, shows a section of the road and rail connection from Standerton to Newcastle via Volksrust. *(Courtesy Map Collection, University of the Witwatersrand Library)*

After their hasty departure from Standerton at two o'clock on 11 October 1899, the day on which war was declared, the marchers crossed the Katbosch Spruit about ten kilometres out of town. Here Marwick warned them that the march would have to continue until well after midnight. This photograph, taken in 1894, shows NZASM officials inspecting the construction of the bridge across the spruit. *(Courtesy Transnet Heritage Library)*

which had been bought from Field Cornet Boshoff to be slaughtered to provide the 'gang' with some food. Before they set off, smaller pieces were sold to the marchers.

Marwick went to Corporal Williams: 'We must go on ahead to see General Joubert at Sandspruit.'

After a ride of five hours they arrived at Sandspruit, to find that General Joubert had left for Volksrust.

'The Boers told us that the camp at Sandspruit was struck yesterday. The Irish Brigade [who volunteered on the Boer side] were just moving off to Volksrust when we came up. There were about sixty-eight men,' Marwick recorded.

Everyone was extremely tense. For the first time on the journey Marwick himself was in danger. He was treated like the enemy by local Boers when he went to the Sandspruit station to send a telegram.

'Why should we send your telegram?,' the Dutch official asked insultingly.

Marwick recalled: 'He refused point blank to take the telegram from me for no apparent reason other than that I spoke in the English language.'

'Is that Englishman going to Natal?' a Boer from one of the commandos asked Corporal Williams.

'Yes.'

'Well then, shoot him before he crosses the border.'

'But he is sticking up for his country just as you would do for the Transvaal. Give him a fair chance,' Williams replied. Curiously enough this reply pacified the official.

Eventually Marwick and Williams were allowed to return to the 'gang' which had come within three miles of Sandspruit station. They made camp, but many marchers who had fallen sick, slept far behind the main group. They could not manage the last two miles which separated them from the main camp.

The marchers had to endure the night on an inhospitable veld. Later Francis Harrison described an area made up of 'interminable and monotonous' plains. 'The effect produced, at a cursory glance over the land, is that of a level table like a billiard table. At intervals in this vast prairie are to be found huge ravines – without anything on the surface indicative of their presence – in which armies of 20 000 men or more are swallowed up with ease. The country in summer is covered with grass ... and the appearance of the vegetation in that season, when thundershowers are frequent, is by no means unattractive.' By no means unattractive, perhaps, unless one is caught in such a storm without any shelter after almost a week on the road.

That night the marchers came up against the forces of nature. Marwick recalled: 'A heavy downpour of rain came on. Before morning the place was practically under water. A large number of natives were suffering severely from exposure.'

Not very far away, the commando to which Reitz belonged was caught in the same storm: 'We spent an unhappy night in the rain. We had neither tents nor overcoats, so we sat on ant-heaps, or lay in the mud, snatching what sleep we could. It was our first introduction to the real hardships of war, and our martial feelings were considerably damped by the time the downpour ceased at daybreak. When it was light we moved out, shivering and hungry, for it was too wet to build fires.'

FRIDAY 13 OCTOBER 1899
Near Sandspruit the march was in serious trouble. The men were suffering as much as the commandos. And at any moment they could be trapped by an army on the move. Many marchers could no longer keep up with the march and to top it all, they had spent a night getting soaked in the storm.

Early that morning Marwick spoke to his colleagues. 'We must get the natives to march before making their usual meal. Mr Connorton, ride on to see General Joubert at Volksrust. Mr Wheelwright, proceed with the main body of natives. I will ride back to bring up the sick. I will try to have them entrained at Sandspruit.'

Marwick managed to get twenty men onto a train at the station. 'The Netherlands Railway officials kindly permitted them to travel to the border free of charge,' he later reported to the others. Here the six mounted policemen were due to leave the march.

By nine o'clock Marwick had overtaken the main body of marchers. A quarter of an hour later they arrived at Volksrust.

'Halt!' officers at the Vrederechter's office ordered Marwick.

'I would like to see General Joubert. I wish to present my papers to him. We also need to obtain food supplies,' Marwick said to an adjutant of the ZAR 'Staats Artillerie'. He looked at the officer. 'But I am sure I have made your acquaintance before. You used to be a captain with the Umvoti Mounted Rifles in Natal.'

'Come. Come to my tent. Let me get you something to eat and drink,' the officer replied and treated them with the warmest hospitality,

It was going to be a strange war. At Sandspruit Marwick had met a brigade of Irishmen who had volunteered to fight on the Boer side. One can understand why the Irish, who had been fighting against the English in Ireland for hundreds of years, would fight with the Boers. Now, he encountered a soldier who had been trained in the Umvoti Mounted Rifles, in the British colony Natal along British military lines, and who was also fighting on the side of the Boers. His pro-Boer sentiments were easy to comprehend. Despite the British character of most of Natal, he came from a district that ever since the 1840s had had a strong Dutch-speaking community.[7]

Two hours later, at about eleven o'clock, the last of the straggling marchers – still almost seven thousand men, women and children – walked into Volksrust. The group was almost as big as the Boer army which had passed through the previous day!

Volksrust was a tiny village which owed its existence to a brisk trade in wool and the main railway line from Natal to the Rand. It consisted of about 250 houses built mostly from wood and corrugated iron. 'Its only ornament is a stone monument, erected in memory of those who fell in this vicinity in the Anglo-Boer War of 1881,' Francis Harrison remarked in 1903.

At Volksrust Marwick addressed the great crowd: 'I have bad news. All trains

The Transvaal Hotel, Volksrust, which would have been visited by members of General Joubert's army as they moved through the village. *(Courtesy Transnet Heritage Library)*

Volksrust consisted of about 250 houses, built mostly from wood and corrugated iron. The village owed its existence to the Natal railway line which terminated at Charlestown, just across the border with Natal. Before the completion of the railway line, passengers were taken from Volksrust by stagecoach to Johannesburg. *(Courtesy Transnet Heritage Library)*

into Natal have been discontinued. It will be necessary to walk all the way to Newcastle, if not further, to reach railway communication. Do not turn aside while we pass through Volksrust and Charlestown. Charlestown is no longer occupied by English inhabitants. Take care that no looting is carried on. As we walk past them we shall salute General and Mrs Joubert. We will salute them when I raise my hat to say good-bye. Then we will proceed across the border. We will outspan after passing through Charlestown.'

General Joubert, who had commanded the Boers at their victory at Majuba in 1881, was now an old man. All along he had been sympathetic towards Marwick and Marwick now acknowledged his assistance. Joubert himself did not want unnecessary bloodshed, looting and plundering, or unnecessary requisitioning of provisions by his commandos once they entered Natal. He was especially indignant when he heard that some commandos had requisitioned cattle from local black farmers. He declared, 'Such people deserve the gallows because they betray our country and our great cause in an indirect way. It is now time to give the natives something, rather than to take something from them.'[8]

He could, however, not prevent such deeds everywhere. The Boers occupied Laing's Nek, the only direct route down the Drakensberg mountain. Marwick had heard that the Boers had looted Legge's store on the way, and that the Belgrave Hotel and other places had been broken into.

Movement on the road down the mountain was made more difficult by continuous drizzle, intermittent showers and thick mist. The Boer artillery horses had great difficulty in pulling cannons and ammunition wagons up the steep Drakensberg foothills overlooking the road from Natal. Deneys Reitz recalled the descent of the Boers: 'Our road lay

83

General Joubert, his staff and a black servant (on the left). This photograph was taken at Newcastle on 17 October 1899, four days after their encounter with the marchers at Volksrust. These men were probably in attendance when General Joubert took the salute as Marwick and the Zulus marched past. *(Courtesy MuseuMAfricA)*

between high mountains, and the rain came down in torrents. Far away to our right and left we caught an occasional glimpse of other forces marching through the mist, also making slow progress over heavy country. We did not cross the border, but kept to a parallel road, and by dark we halted at a dismal spot, soon trampled into a quagmire by a multitude of horses. Again it rained all night, and again we had no fires, and had to appease our hunger by munching biltong from our saddle-bags. It was a severe first test, for in addition to the rain, a cold wind blew from the great Drakensberg range, cutting through us.'

The marchers were suffering as much as, if not more than, the commandos.

They had no horses. They had no food. They had been on the road for almost a week. In addition, they were famished. They needed food before they could even try to continue down the mountain. Marwick went into Charlestown and enquired about provisions.

Situated about four kilometres from Volksrust and at the furthest limit of the north-western frontier between Natal and the ZAR, Charlestown owed its existence to the railway line which linked Durban with Johannesburg. Before the railway line was completed in 1895, Charlestown served as the terminus where passengers had to change to stage-coaches for the rest of the journey to the gold-fields.

A contemporary picture of a farm near Volksrust, nestled in the foothills of the Drakensberg. After the rolling plains between Standerton and Volksrust, the landscape through which the marchers moved became more rugged. *(Courtesy Transnet Heritage Library)*

At Charlestown, two black men who worked for a Mr S F Higgens took Marwick to a house where fifty bags of mealies were stored. 'We will sell you twenty-one bags of these mealies on our employer's behalf. The price of the mealies is one pound per muid,' Marwick was told.

Enough money was collected from the marchers to pay for the mealies.

Marwick did not realise it, but he and the men were about to commence the most dangerous and exhausting leg of the long march.

While the marchers were at Charlestown, the first battery of the Boer artillery was ordered to take the main road to Newcastle. The marchers followed these Boer commandos down Laing's Nek, past Mount Prospect where in 1881 the peace treaty had been signed after the Battle of Majuba, and where a number of British soldiers who had died during the First Anglo-Boer War lay buried.

At the bottom of the mountain Wheelwright, who was leading the marchers, was stopped by the Boer commandos.

'You are ordered to turn back immediately,' declared Commandant S P E Trichardt. 'From this point onwards you cannot be allowed to march ahead of the Boer commandos.'

'What should we do?' Marwick, Connorton and Wheelwright asked one another in desperation. Just then the ex-captain of the Umvoti Mounted Rifles whom Marwick had met at Volksrust again appeared on the scene. Marwick explained the situation.

'We have seven thousand natives on the verge of starvation. They are treading on the heels of three thousand armed Boers. This constitutes the elements of a great massacre of defenceless people,' Marwick implored. 'All the danger could be averted by simply allowing us to pass through. You are on good terms with Commandant Trichardt. Ride with me to General Colley's old camp at Mount Prospect. The artillery has halted there for the night. Speak to him,' he urged him.

Marwick waited anxiously where the British had camped before the battle of Majuba while the ex-captain spoke to Commandant Trichardt. Trichardt changed his mind and agreed: 'Tell Lieutenant de Jager, the Chief of the Battery, to let Marwick pass with the natives. Endorse the safe-conduct papers accordingly.'

At about eight o'clock that evening, with his safe-conduct papers duly signed, Marwick returned to the Mount Prospect

A bird's-eye view of the railway line as it winds down the Drakensberg between Volksrust and Ingogo. From the highveld the marchers descended rapidly down the mountains into Natal. *(Courtesy Transnet Heritage Library)*

stream. Here the group told him that the Boer transport officers had commandeered 400 of them. The men had to assist in dragging two guns and six ammunition wagons up the hill, which owing to the heavy rain the mules had been unable to negotiate.

'We are drenched,' the men said. 'We are thoroughly tired out by this effort.'

'Let us sleep here and proceed before daybreak,' Marwick suggested.

Everyone at the Mount Prospect stream camp spent a miserable night. A Boer eyewitness later recalled: 'It was bitterly cold and wet, because it drizzled continuously. Wet and cold we walked around to see how our fellow combatants were doing. Here and there we found a small group of Boers around a small kettle of water placed on the fire, waiting for wonderful irreplaceable coffee to relieve their suffering.'[9] At least they had some coffee and biltong on which to chew.

SATURDAY 14 OCTOBER 1899

At four o'clock in the morning the marchers left their camp. 'We started off without food. We passed through the Boer lines at sunrise. We walked through to Newcastle without a halt,' Marwick recalled a few days later.

Marwick's brief report gives little indication of the rough terrain through which the 'gang' had to march. They were surrounded by high mountains. From the Ingogo station they could see the three Drakensberg peaks, Inkwelo, Amajuba and Pogwana, all about 2 000 metres high.

Francis Harrison's 1903 description for the benefit of tourists gives some idea of the hardship the marchers had to endure: 'Not only are the mountains of special attraction to the tourist, but the Buffalo River which formerly divided Natal from the Transvaal on the east, and flows through a wild and tangled country, is peculiarly interesting to the portrayer of weird and lonely scenes.'

Newcastle, Marwick's next destination, was again according to Harrison, 'from a picturesque and residential point of view, one of the nicest in the colony [Natal], the climate being most invigorating'. The town had about 7 000 black and white inhabitants. In July 1899 a new town hall 'with clock and chimes' was inaugurated to commemorate Queen Victoria's diamond jubilee.

At Newcastle Marwick approached the magistrate, Mr Otter Jackson. 'Can you kindly arrange for the rationing of the natives? By four this afternoon we will resume our journey.'

That afternoon, as they were leaving, Wheelwright and Marwick turned back to say goodbye to the magistrate. There they found that the war had caught up with them. Commandant De Witt Hamer from the Boer camp was with the magistrate.

'I have come to inform you of the advance of the Transvaal forces,' announced the commandant. 'We intend to occupy the town before nightfall.'

As soon as Marwick and Wheelwright heard the commandant, they left the town. They caught up with the men near Ingagane station, some twelve kilometres outside Newcastle. Behind them the three Drakensberg peaks towered, silent witnesses yet again to a war about to be fought.

Marwick continued to Garden's Mission Station where the group spent the night. The marchers had now entered the no-man's land between the two enemy lines. The British army was encamped around Dundee, just south of their camp-site.

SUNDAY 15 OCTOBER 1899

'We proceed at daylight. We cannot give you time to cook a meal,' Marwick ordered the marchers once again. They had to put as much distance as possible between themselves and the Boer forces. At least twelve hours of marching followed.

Two incidents marred the last part of the march. At Ingogo a Mr Oliver Davis and at Dannhauser a Mr H Caister sold liquor to the marchers. When Marwick warned Caister not to do so, he replied laconically, 'We must make hay while the sun shines.'[10]

'I understand that their places were looted by the natives to whom they supplied drink. Two bottles of brandy found by me in possession of natives coming out of Caister's store were handed in at the Attorney-General's office yesterday,' Marwick reported later.

During the day the group split up. About three thousand people took the road that turned off to Zululand. At Ingangane station about two thousand took the Ladysmith road. Other marchers managed to reach their homes in the Newcastle district. By five o'clock the thousand or more people who had remained on the march arrived at Hattingh's Spruit station.

Hattingh's Spruit station was an insignificant siding with branch lines connecting the Navigation, St George's and Glencoe collieries. A small hotel was situated next to the siding. Here there were trains available to transport the remainder of Marwick's group. However, unlike on the NZASM trains, it would not be a free ride. The marchers had to pay for their own transport home.

'Trains are available for those wishing to proceed coastwards,' Marwick declared. 'You will be charged £1 each to cover the cost of the trains.' It seemed a great deal of money: just before the war, a train ticket from Richmond, south of Pietermaritzburg, to Johannesburg cost £2 1s. 6d., an enormous chunk out of a monthly wage of about £3.

After ten gruelling days on the road, having achieved a remarkable feat, Marwick knew that no money would be forthcoming from his bosses in Pietermaritzburg. Whereas the NZASM had been willing to come to the aid of the marchers, neither the Natal government nor the Natal railway officials seemed to be willing to put up any money towards Marwick's rescue operation. Throughout the journey he had to keep his bosses warning in mind to spend as little money as possible.

Marwick's report on how the march finally ended was terse – as if it was too much of an effort to say much more: 'The valediction of the natives to us when they dispersed bore pleasing testimony to the fact that one and all appreciated our remaining with them when they were at a loss to help themselves. I believe there is widespread thankfulness for our having been brought safely through.'

Chapter 7

BACK HOME IN PIETERMARITZBURG

The train left Hattingh's Spruit on Sunday evening and arrived at Pietermaritzburg station the following day, Monday 16 October 1899. Marwick was met by his brother, Alan, the Natal Secretary of Native Affairs, the Honourable F Moor and Under-Secretary O S Samuelson, as well as many local people who had heard of the march.

Marwick was praised widely: in Great Britain, in the newspapers, by friends and by the Prime Minister of Natal, who sent the following following telegram to Glencoe station: 'Heartiest congratulations from us all on your safe arrival after your grand march. Your self-sacrificing conduct has our highest appreciation. The Governor especially desires me to convey to you his warm appreciation and approval of your conduct in the matter.'[1]

Marwick was the hero of the day. His offer to resign was never mentioned again.

In Great Britain, Joseph Chamberlain, Secretary of State for the Colonies, had been fully informed of the march of the Zulus. On 18 November 1899 he received

Pietermaritzburg station where Marwick was welcomed by his brother Alan and various officials of the Natal Native Affairs Department after the completion of the march. The station was obviously the hub of a busy and thriving town. *(Courtesy Transnet Heritage Library)*

The Prime Minister of Natal sent Marwick a telegram of congratulations, which he received at Glencoe station. This copy of the telegram was kept by Marwick amongst his papers, which were donated to the Killie Campbell Africana Library by his daughter in the 1970s. *(Courtesy Killie Campbell Africana Library)*

copies of all the telegrams which had been sent to and from Johannesburg before the start of the march.

Marwick was back in Pietermaritzburg. He had received his welcome and telegrams of congratulations, but his work was not done. He was ordered to write a detailed report on the march, which he started without delay on 19 October when he received his orders. On 20 October, the Principal Under-Secretary in London asked when the report would be finished! He was told that Marwick began writing the report 'on 20 October at seven o'clock and has been at it since seven this morning without intermission'.

Marwick put a great deal of effort into his report. He soon completed it, and by 23 October the Natal Governor, Sir Walter Hely-Hutchinson, could send copies to the State Secretary in London, and the High Commissioner in Cape Town. He reported to Mr Chamberlain in Great Britain: 'Mr Marwick informs me that, although the party suffered considerable hardship, no life was lost on the way; but one native, who was in a weak state on leaving Johannesburg, reached Hattingh Spruit in an apparently dying state.'

He added, 'I have expressed to Mr Marwick my high appreciation of his conduct, and have submitted that it deserves the favourable notice of His Majesty's Government.'[2]

On 23 November, Chamberlain received Marwick's long report on the march which described the progress of the 'gang' from day to day. Chamberlain commented, 'I have perused this account with interest, and I agree with the opinion expressed by you that Mr Marwick and the others responsible for carrying out the arrangement for the return of the natives deserve great credit for its success.'[3]

Marwick, whilst in Pietermaritzburg, had his photograph taken by the photographers W Watson & Robertson on Chapel Street. The man in the photograph on page 92 does not look as though he had marched for more than ten days! Marwick wears a stiff white collar, a fashionable tie and a dark suit. His moustache is twirled according to the latest fashion. In one hand he carries a pith helmet such as Londoners would buy for an African safari. In the other hand he holds a fly whisk, the traditional symbol of a man of power in Zulu society. With these two objects in his hands he seems to be saying that he is equally at home in the British and the Zulu worlds.

One detail in the photograph, however, portrays how hard Marwick had worked to earn all the fame and praise heaped on him. He is not completely the dandy. His shoes, the same pair that he had been wearing when the picture of him on page 63 was taken, probably in Johannesburg some time before the march,

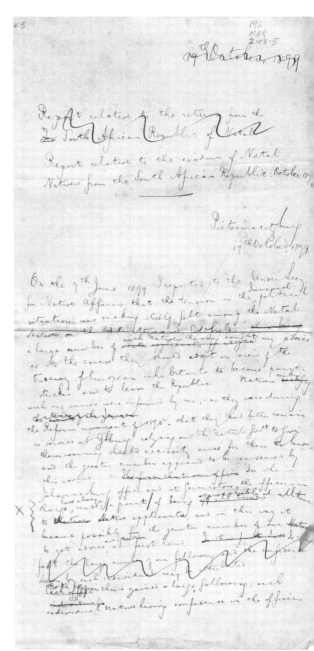

The first page of the handwritten draft of the report which Marwick began to write on 20 October 1899, five days after the completion of the march. From his many corrections it is clear that he put a great deal of effort into the task. In 1900 the report was published in the *Blue Book, [Cd 43], Further Correspondence Relating to Affairs in South Africa.* *(Courtesy Killie Campbell Africana Library)*

John Sidney Marwick, photographed in Pietermaritz-burg after the march. The state of his shoes, in contrast to his clothes, provides evidence of the long march he had just completed. *(Courtesy Clare Rossouw)*

Marwick (middle) with his two colleagues, Connorton and Wheelwright, who worked with him on the Reef and who accompanied him on the march from Johannesburg to Natal. *(Courtesy Clare Rossouw)*

urgently needed to be repaired. There are gaping holes at the toes of the shoes, and they have lost much of their original form. The shoes, it would seem, reveal why this smartly dressed young man in the picture had earned the nickname 'Muhle', which means good or kind.

In another picture we see the three comrades, Marwick, Connorton and Wheelwright. The three dashing young men are sporting suits, waistcoats and bow ties. The photograph, too, betrays little of the hardship which they had experienced.

Marwick was praised and honoured. Nevertheless, he had lost his job in

Johannesburg with the outbreak of the war. Early in December 1899, like other patriotic young Natalians, Marwick enlisted. He was immediately appointed as an administrator in the Native Affairs Intelligence Department. He was posted to the Department's division in Frere in central Natal where he was given the job of assembling black men to work as non-combatants for the army. The task of this Native Labour Corps was to dig trenches, to help with the transport of goods and weapons, and to do general 'fatigue' duties.

Many of the one thousand men whom Marwick hired had been on the march with him. Not unreasonably, they saw the war as an opportunity to earn some good money. During the war black men sometimes earned up to a pound a week, in contrast to British soldiers who were paid only a shilling a day.

The Native Labour Corps was attached to General Redvers Buller's army and was under the command of General Wolf-Murray. Marwick was to work with J F E Barne, who was in charge of the corps, and a Mr Hope Pool, who was the superintendent. As administrator of the corps, Marwick was given the job of maintaining the corps at full strength, of preventing or settling disputes, and of dealing with 'detail questions which are certain to arise'.[4]

Marwick had become so well-known in Natal that when the *Times of Natal* reported on Marwick's formation of the corps on 14 December 1899, it called it 'a feat quite equal to the splendid march'. In a curriculum vitae which Marwick wrote after the war, he mentioned the work he had done. 'During the war I raised and commanded a Native Labour Corps of many thousands of men for which I received honourable mention by the late General Sir Redvers Buller.' After the war, when Marwick was again looking for work, Lieutenant Colonel H G Morgan, Director of Supplies of the Chief of Staff of the Natal Field Force, supplied Marwick with this testimonial: 'Mr Marwick has performed most invaluable service whilst employed under me, not only as in charge of the Native Labour Corps, but also in assisting me in taking descriptions of captured stock, herding and generally looking after them until disposed of. His popularity with the natives is almost extraordinary and without his influence we would never have got the natives to accompany the troops at the front. He recruited the corps (a thousand strong) entirely by himself in December last.'[5]

It would seem that Wheelwright had also joined the Native Labour Corps. Once while at work a photograph was taken of the two men on horseback.

Marwick and Wheelwright on horseback whilst working with the Native Labour Corps in Natal during the war. The Corps was responsible for doing general fatigue duties such as digging trenches and transporting goods. It is not known where this photograph was taken. *(Courtesy Killie Campbell Africana Library)*

By the end of 1900 Marwick had found work with the British Native Intelligence Department in Pretoria. Here he did much the same work as he had done before the war in Pretoria – looking after the interests of the men who worked for him. In September 1900 Marwick forwarded the request of Abram Tombisa to Captain A Hughes. Tombisa wrote:

I beg to lay this humble petition before you for kind consideration. I have faithfully served the Department of Native Intelligence on the field for three months with praise from the officer commanding. I return and find my family suffering from want of food because they are not able to buy any for their money. I therefore beg to be allowed the same facilities buying flour and other articles that are supplied to Boer families from the commissariat in consideration of my humble services to the British Government.

Like thousands of others, Tombisa's family was suffering the consequences of the war which was raging around them. We do not know whether Tombisa did manage to get food for his family or not. However, in October he had also applied for but was refused permission to leave the camp where he was stationed.[6]

At the end of the war Marwick headed back to Johannesburg, this time as a Native Commissioner with the newly-formed British-run civil service of the Transvaal Colony. Whereas before the war he received a salary of £300 per annum, he now asked for and was given a salary of £900. This was indeed a very good salary. Marwick was appointed from 1 January 1902 and held the position until 1905.

In November 1901, Marwick returned to Natal where he married Miss Edith Rowe, daughter of the late Reverend S Evans Rowe. According to her granddaughter, Clare Rossouw, 'Grandmother was a very beautiful woman, a great beauty of the family and even of Natal. Granddad used to go to church – her father's church – in order to stare at her. Mr Rowe would invite the congregation to tea after the service. Granddad went to some of those teas and he met her there. And he stole one of the pictures of her on the family mantelpiece! He actually took it. There was a letter from him, admitting this, saying that he was sure that the Rowes must be looking for the picture, and that he had actually been the person who nicked it.

'I think he fell in love with her when she was still a schoolgirl, from what was said, but I'm not sure.

'The Rowes came from quite high-born English gentry. The five daughters were all well-educated and were sent back to England to be brought out at court. During the time my grandmother was away, she and granddad wrote to each other regularly.

'My mother later destroyed those letters; she felt they were very personal. She thought only things of public interest should be kept.'

Some time after the march Marwick gave his fiancée a tiny gold ring to commemorate the march. The inscription on the inside reads, 'Edith from Sidney, Oct 7 1899 – Oct 16 1899'. The ring is now in the possession of his granddaughter Clare Rossouw.

It was a sumptuous wedding that took place in the Wesleyan Church in Pietermaritzburg in November 1901. It was attended by some 250 people, with the reception held at the Masonic Hall. Many men who had taken part in the march also came to pay their respects at the wedding. The church 'was beautifully decorated with ferns and arum lilies, which had been brought into town by the natives to show their respect for Mr Marwick, and to bear witness that his service to them in leading seven thousand of them safely through the Transvaal through the Boer lines back to their homes two years ago, was not forgotten. Since that time he has been a power among the natives and they even asked to be allowed to execute a war dance on his wedding day! This offer, though much appreciated, was declined; nevertheless large numbers of natives congregated round the church doors hours before the ceremony in order to obtain a glimpse of their hero,' a local newspaper reported.

According to the same report, the bride wore a 'very pretty white merve silk dress, trimmed with real Honiton lace and orange blossoms, and carried a bouquet of white roses, lilies and carnations, and as she joined her bridegroom at the altar she looked the personification of radiant happiness and loving trust'. The glowing description of the bridesmaids, the groom's presents to his bride, the bride's going-away dress, the important guests who were present and the presents they gave – all were duly noted, especially the silver apostle spoons and sugar tongs from Sir Albert Hime, the Natal Prime Minister.

After their wedding, Marwick and Edith moved to Johannesburg. Theirs was not a long marriage as Edith died in 1907, some weeks after the birth of her daughter, Vivian – Marwick's only child. Marwick remarried more than twenty years later.

What happened to the workers who had marched home with Marwick? Clare Rossouw remembers that when she was a child, 'There were always large delegations of Zulu people coming to see granddad. He had a number of small, low, wooden chairs in his office where he and his visitors sat. I remember, when we were young, if we came into his office where he and his Zulu friends were talking, and if we were tall enough to be standing above them, granddad insisted that we go down on our knees, so that we would not be towering over people who were our seniors and – as he pointed out – our social betters. His visitors were often chiefs or even royalty. All his life, Zulu people included granddad in their *indabas* and asked him to settle disputes.'

She also vividly describes her grandfather's funeral in Pietermaritzburg in 1958 when the Zulus came to pay their last respects:

'Peka ka Dinizulu came to granddad's funeral and he did the praise song for granddad. He was Cethswayo's nephew and he was a friend of my grandfather until granddad died. Peka was younger than granddad. We had a Christian burial and all the Zulus sat around, and then afterwards we stepped back, and Peka came in his royal leopard skins and with his spear and his huge white shield with the black interlacing and gave honour to granddad.

'It was wonderful how many people come to be with us for granddad's funeral. As many as there were, they came to his farm and they just sat quietly. My

Peka ka Dinizulu, here in regimental dress, participated in the march and remained a friend to Marwick until Marwick's death in 1958. *(Courtesy Clare Rossouw)*

step-grandmother ordered beasts to be killed and porridge to be made. And through her *induna* she spoke to the people gathered there. She said that we were a long way from Pietermaritzburg where my grandfather would be buried and that she would be happy to hire buses to take them there. But the people objected. They said: "No, we have come to honour the *inkosi* and we will walk from here."

'And so they did. The funeral took place late in the afternoon so that they could walk there. They set off early in the morning. When we drove into Pietermaritzburg, there were so many people sitting on the hillside of the cemetery, just quietly waiting. When Peka spoke they all stood up. Whenever he paused in his stories of my grandfather, he would look towards the people. Then they would acknowledge what he had said. They "hayesed" and "bayeted" so that there was a huge wave of sound, a sort of agreement to everything that the prince said. It was very beautiful and it was very comforting.'

Marwick was well remembered by the Zulus. But he himself seldom spoke of the march during his lifetime. Clare Rossouw tells the following story: 'Granddad did not tell me about the march himself. He lived very much in the present; he always told stories to entertain people or to make us laugh. And I think that he was modest. He felt that the march was a great achievement, but he didn't speak about it. I only ever heard two of his sisters speak of it. His eldest sister, Edith Clarke, wrote an account of it and gave a talk on the radio about it. She was the eldest daughter, so she must have been aware when granddad did the march. The other person who spoke about it was his youngest sister, Phyllis Marwick. She never married but brought up my mother when my grandmother died.

'Granddad didn't talk about the march, but auntie Phyllis did. It's interesting now to read the accounts of it, because family legend was rather different.

'The family legend was quite romantic, actually. Auntie always said that the king asked granddad to bring the Zulus back. That he, the king, was worried and that he called granddad and said could he, would he, do this.

'And granddad said, "I'm not sure that I can do it, because the people on the gold-fields won't know me. They won't realise that I am your ambassador. I need a member of your family with me." It was then that Peka ka Dinizulu said that he would go with granddad.

'Peka and my grandfather went to Johannesburg. They went to the mine managers, because most of the Zulus were working on the mines, on contract. Peka and my grandfather wanted assurances from the mine managers, auntie said, that they would waive the contracts and allow the people to go home. It was important that they would not be regarded as criminals, running away from an undertaking. Once the managers had agreed, Peka and grandfather went to Pretoria to ask for a safe conduct and permission to go through the war-torn area. And eventually that was agreed to. Auntie always said that it was the President, Kruger himself, who agreed to it.

'Granddad and his brother, Alan, had

met the President before. Granddad had introduced himself then. He felt very strongly that you should make yourself known to people in case you had to deal with them, and they wanted to know who you were, and whether you were a trustworthy kind of person.

'Auntie mentioned several things about the march that she repeated quite often whenever people asked her about it. She said, for instance, that Peka and granddad held meetings, and a lot of people came. And then they started laying down the conditions of the march.

'They said to the people, "The white people are fighting between themselves and the whole country is in a state of war. Everybody is nervous, and so nobody will march armed. You will have to give every stick, every assegai, every shield, every battle axe, every gun to Mr Marwick. Nobody may have arms of any kind. And even if we are attacked we must not retaliate. If we are hurt, if the white people are frightened and they shoot at us and some of us are hurt, we must pick up the people who are hurt and carry them until we are past the people who are frightened and attacking us. Then we will attend to their wounds.

'"We do not want any fighting and stealing amongst people on the march. All the money is to be given in. We will keep records – we will write down what each one of you gives in, money as well as weapons. At the end of the march you will get them back.

'"If you have any horses, mules or donkeys, or carts or anything else, you will have to give them in. Because we will need them to carry food and people who are old, sick or weak, or women and children who need transport."

'And a lot of people left the meetings. Many people said, "Oh no, *hayi*, that's no good. If we have to give in our weapons and our money, and other people are going to use our transport, then we are not going."

'And so the number diminished considerably. But there were many that stayed. Auntie used to talk about six thousand people marching. I saw some accounts which said there were ten thousand people.

'According to auntie, granddad said that twice on the march they were attacked by farmers who were horrified to see this huge *impi*. People were hurt, but not severely. The other marchers did exactly what they had been instructed to do. They picked up the injured people and they carried them a little further on. Then they put them down and dressed their wounds. But nobody was killed.

'One of the people who worked with granddad was a Zulu man called Mr Solomon. According to Mr Solomon, the Zulus themselves said that granddad was very brave on the march. Several times, when white men were advancing on

them with guns, granddad stopped the marchers and said, "You sit down, wait. I will go."

'And although the white men were threatening to shoot, granddad walked right up to them, and spoke to them and showed them the passes which the government had stamped and sealed. The marchers were amazed at his courage in the face of aggression. And that sort of thing happened quite often.

'The other thing that the marchers remembered him for was his willingness to share their hardships. Granddad didn't live in luxury on the march. He marched with the people and when the food was getting low, he shared with them. They saw what he ate, that he didn't go away and put up a tent and eat vast quantities of food. When the food was short, they were all short.

'This was not first-hand from granddad. This account was from his sister. After the march, when granddad was back in Natal, he went to speak to the king to say, "The work is done, it is completed."

'Legends grow up – and they grow quickly, as you can hear from the account that I grew up with,' Clare Rossouw concluded.

Chapter 8

WHAT PEOPLE SAID ABOUT THE MARCH

The messages of congratulation and newspaper articles written about the march were important to Marwick. He kept them all very carefully amongst his papers. But many details reported by Marwick were changed as the story was retold in the newspapers.

On 18 October 1899 the London newspaper, *Daily Mail*, published a report on the march written by their correspondent in Durban: 'Mr Marwick's march over a distance of 400 miles through mostly hostile territory is an extraordinary feat … The "boys" are mainly Zulus, and therefore used to discipline, but the marshalling, the feeding and the maintenance of order among such a huge number is proof of organising and administrative power which is rare … The spectacle of this army of returning mining boys with their boots slung round their necks and their pannikins on their backs, shouting, screaming and dancing, must have been very weird.'

In Marwick's papers, clippings of other newspapers articles with headings such as 'A Plucky Son of Plucky Little Natal' were found. The reporter became quite lyrical:

'Mr J S Marwick, who arrived yesterday, after his arduous and plucky march down from Johannesburg with 5,000 Natal and Zululand natives, certainly deserves to go down in history as one of the heroes of this campaign. From accounts that reach us through natives his conduct is beyond praise, and his courage is of the very highest order. They point to Heaven, when describing his courage and say that he must be a supreme chief from thence. Time after time the Boers used insult and abuse, and threatened to shoot him where he stood, so the natives say, yet he never flinched, nor failed to give them back with dignity the words of a man who knows no fear, and who requires no "gallery" to stimulate him with applause. Practically alone and unarmed, he would hurl back defiance in the teeth of his cowardly abusers and say: I know that I am powerless now, but when I have entered Natal with my "boys" I will return and fight you. There are not many instances in history of brave, provocative words, so bravely spoken – under threat of immediate death – to those in power to execute the threat. Young Mr J S Marwick is a plucky son of "Plucky little Natal", and his mother-land is immensely proud of him.'[1]

Another article entitled 'A Memorable March' in which Marwick himself was interviewed, stated:

'When the history of the part played by Natal in connection with the Boer War of 1899 comes to be written, a prominent place will have to be accorded to the feat accomplished by Mr J S Marwick, the representative at Johannesburg of the Department of the Secretary of Native Affairs, in bringing a body of Natal and Zululand natives numbering at least 8,000 from the Rand through the Transvaal – in fact through one of the chief Boer strongholds – into their own country. The achievement is one which speaks volumes for the pluck, determination, and tact of the young Natalian who planned, organised, and carried out the undertaking.'[2]

On 1 December 1899 an admirer, Mr N D Hole, from Bristol in Great Britain, who seemed to have known Marwick in Johannesburg before the war, wrote the following letter to him:

'Read of your plucky march, have enclosed copy printed by the *Daily Mail's Weekly*. My comment is, "Well done." I presume Ivy [a common acquaintance] was with you, if so please tell him when you see him that I envied him the chance. I shall have to include Moses to your other titles, Bayete, etc, etc.'

Hole included the article entitled 'A Modern Moses'. It painted the march in very heroic colours and many facts were exaggerated to impress the readers in Great Britain:

'From kraal to kraal the story of Marwick's achievement in bringing 6,000 natives through the Transvaal wilderness into Natal, their Canaan, is circulating. It will be handed down from generation to generation; it will live. But what is the story?'

The article then summarises the story, but adds a few extra, dramatic details about Marwick's plans 'for the deliverance of his people':

'No food supplies were obtainable on the road, thunderstorms were encountered at various points of the weary march, and every Boer township had to be approached with extreme caution, the chief danger feared being a sudden attack from a Boer commando, through misconception of the character of the expedition ... It was a splendid achievement, admirably planned and carried out, and no brighter example of British pluck and determination is to be found in the annals of Natal.'[3]

Soon after the march, writers began to add some of their own interpretations of the story to add flavour. Early in 1900 the writer of a story in the British magazine, *Leisure Hour*, substituted imagination for fact and showed clearly that he had little knowledge of the real events of the march. He described the Zulu miners as 'the vast crowd of simple, child-like, helpless natives'. He also put words in Louis de Souza's mouth which Marwick did not report. When he heard what Marwick planned to do, De Souza allegedly exclaimed, 'By road! It will be leading them to certain death! Our commandos will certainly fire on them when they see a large body of blacks advancing on them.'[4]

100

Also in 1900, Clement H Stott published a book called *The Boer Invasion of Natal* in which he described what he thought the Zulus would have felt on getting close to the border. 'On nearing the Natal border the Natives began to exhibit signs of fear owing to the insults and threatening attitude of the Boer commandos, and it was not until the border at Charlestown was crossed that their fears were allayed. They now realised that they were under protection of the "Great White Queen" [Queen Victoria].'[5]

Some forty years later, journalists were still using their imagination. J P Cope was political correspondent of the *Natal Mercury*. In an undated report entitled 'The Epic March of the Ten Thousand', he described what he thought the march would have looked like: 'At night time the fires of the little groups of Natives scattered far and wide over the veldt, flickered like the lights of a city.' He concluded, 'The story of the trek, coloured and magnified with the years, is to this day told in the kraals of Zululand by a few grey-beards still living who took part in the adventure.'[6]

Many people referred to the march during Marwick's long career, which later included his election as Member of Parliament for Illovo. But slowly the march was forgotten by the general public. People who had been on the march, however, did pass the story on to their children. Once in July 1953 Marwick received a letter from the son of a man who had marched with him.

James Kjokweni Dumakude Mkwanazi wrote: 'It was my privilege to learn of you from my late father, Solashe ka Simangentaba Mkwanazi, who I have reason to believe will be remembered by you. It was he who related to me how a vast multitude of Natal and Zululand natives, including Mntwana Pka ka Siteku and my late father under your able leadership, trekked to Natal from Johannesburg.'[7]

Contrary to many people's predictions after the march, it was not recorded in the official histories written about the war. Neither Leo Amery's *The Times History of the War in South Africa*, written from the British perspective, nor J H Breytenbach's *Geskiedenis van die Tweede Vryheidsoorlog*, written in Afrikaans from the Boer perspective, mentions the march, despite the fact that information on the march had been available since 1900 when Marwick's official report was presented to both houses of the British parliament. The report, *'Further Correspondence relating to Affairs in South Africa' no. Cd. 43*, was published in the official British Blue Books. These Blue Books are available in reference libraries in South African and Great Britain.

Not even people such as Deneys Reitz, who was on commando as the march passed through Volksrust, mentioned the march in his book, *Commando*, which was published in 1929. Neither does Commandant S P E Trichardt in his life story, published in 1975, make mention of his encounter with the marchers at Mount Prospect. J A Mouton, who wrote a biography of General Piet Joubert in 1957, also failed to mention Marwick's meeting with Joubert.

A fragment of the letter written by James Mkwanazi to Marwick in 1953. Mkwanazi refers to the fact that his father had been one of the marchers who completed the epic journey from Johannesburg to Natal with Marwick. *(Courtesy Killie Campbell Africana Library)*

In 1979, in his book *The Boer War*, Thomas Pakenham summarised Marwick's efforts to evacuate the people for whom he was responsible and the subsequent march of the Zulu workers. Pakenham related the story, in some four or five paragraphs, to illustrate the policy of Lord Alfred Milner towards the black people of southern Africa. Milner had been High Commissioner for South Africa and Governor of the Cape Colony from 1897 and played an important role in events which led to the outbreak of the war. Even though Milner had claimed that he wanted 'to secure for natives protection against oppression and wrong', no thought was given to the plight of black people who would be caught up in the war. Pakenham states:

'In terms of human misery, the chief sufferers from the decline and fall of the Rand were not the Uitlanders, but the African mineworkers from Natal and the Cape and the Cape coloured population. They were the "mine-boys" and the artisans. Now their employment had gone. They had little money saved and the Boers were quite prepared to let them starve on the veld. 'Should Milner intervene? It was a question that he could not flinch from.'[8]

In 1982, in his two volumes *Studies in the Social and Economic History of the Witwatersrand, 1886–1914*, Charles van Onselen mentioned the march in passing, when he discussed what happened to kitchenboys, miners and criminals at the outbreak of the war. In 1983, in his book *Black People and the South African War,*

102

1899–1902, Peter Warwick also briefly mentioned the march, as did Diana Cammack in *The Rand at War* in 1990.

More information about the march became available during the 1970s when Marwick's daughter, Vivian Tedder, donated her father's papers to the Killie Campbell Africana Library at the University of Natal in Durban.

'My mother worked at the Killie Campbell Library for many years, until she was seventy. The university had a policy of enforced retirement at seventy,' Clare Rossouw recalled. 'My mother and granddad had a great friendship as well as a working relationship. She was instrumental in giving his papers to Killie Campbell. We spent weeks and weeks going through the papers.

'And eventually we got all these trucks full of things and took them down to Durban,' J S Marwick's granddaughter concluded.

AFTERWORD

In this book, for the first time, material in the Marwick Manuscript Collection at the Killie Campbell Africana Library has been used in conjunction with official reports, academic studies and contemporary photographs, as well as the memories of Clare Rossouw, Marwick's granddaughter, to tell the story of this long march home from Johannesburg to Natal.

The picture is by no means complete. Although many questions have been answered, many still remain. What were the names of the marchers? Who was the little girl with the fever, the man with the amputated toe and the man who fell off the pony? Who were the anonymous Boer farmers, field cornets, traders and shopkeepers who met the marchers along the way? Who was the ex-captain of the Umvoti Mounted Rifles and did he survive the war? What happened to the workers after they reached their homes in Zululand and Natal? What stories did they tell about the march to their children and grandchildren? What happened to Connorton and Wheelwright after the march?

I believe that, with the current retelling of this story, a wider audience will be reached, especially the descendants of those 7 000 workers who began their long march home on 6 October 1899. As it stands my account has had to rely heavily on the reports and recollections of the men who were literate and could record their experiences. The oral testimony which hopefully has survived amongst the descendants of the marchers still needs to be found and recorded. I hope that with this record of the march in words and pictures, people will come forward with more information and their own memories and stories. Only then will a more complete picture of the march emerge.

It is not only Marwick's contribution to the march which should be remembered and honoured. All the workers who joined him on the march, with no guarantee that they would reach home safely, demonstrated that courage, discipline and a communal spirit were essential characteristics to ensure safe passage through a troubled time.

ELSABÉ BRINK
Johannesburg
April 1999

NOTES

PREFACE
Main sources consulted in this chapter
Cammack, Diana (1990) *The Rand at War, 1899-1902: The Witwatersrand and the Anglo-Boer War.* Pietermaritzburg: University of Natal Press.
De Kiewiet, CW (1978) *A History of South Africa, Social and Economic.* Oxford: Oxford University Press.
Harrison, CW Francis (1903) *Natal: An Illustrated Official Railway Guide and Handbook of General Information.* London: Payne Jennings.
Katz, Elaine (1995) 'Outcrop and deep level mining in South Africa before the Anglo-Boer War: re-examining the Blainey thesis', in *The Economic History Review, vol. XLVIII.* 2: May, pp. 304-328.
Pakenham, Thomas (1979) *The Boer War.* Cape Town: Jonathan Ball.
Van Onselen, Charles (1982) *Studies in the Social and Economic History of the Witwatersrand, 1886-1914.* Vols I & II. Johannesburg: Ravan Press.
Warwick, Peter (1982) *Black People and the South African War, 1899-1902.* Johannesburg: Ravan Press.

Notes
[1] Lipp in Cammack, p. 56-57.
[2] Harrison, p. 146.
[3] Pakenham, p. xv.

CHAPTER 1
Main sources consulted in this chapter
Atkins, Keletso E (1989) *The Moon is Dead! Give us our money! The Cultural Origins of an African Work Ethic, Natal, South Africa, 1843-1900.*

Johannesburg: University of Witwatersrand Press.
Guy, Jeff (1982a) 'The destruction and reconstruction of Zulu society' in Marks, S and Rathbone, R, *Industrialisation and Social Change in South Africa: African Class Formation, Culture and Consciousness, 1870-1930.* London: Longman.
Guy, Jeff (1982b) *The Destruction of the Zulu Kingdom.* Johannesburg: Ravan Press.

Notes
[1] Guy (b), p. 49.
[2] Quoted by Atkins, p. 53.

CHAPTER 2
Main sources consulted in this chapter
Coulson, C (1986) *Beaulieu on Illovo, Richmond Natal, Its History and Its People.* Richmond, KwaZulu-Natal: Richmond Woman's League and Institute.
Killie Campbell Africana Library, Marwick Manuscript Collection (hereafter KCM). Information in the following files was used: Files 1-13, 16-18, 21, 34-38, 40, 70-72, 76 and Books 2-3.
Wilson, M & Thompson, L (eds) (1971) *The Oxford History of South Africa, 1870-1966,* Volume II. Oxford: Clarendon Press.

Notes
[1] *Natal Witness Weekly,* 4 October 1913, in Coulson, p. 52.
[2] Ibid, p. 23.
[3] KCM 2566, The early recollections of the late Mrs Thos. Marwick.

[4] I am indebted to Robert Morrell for making his research on the Marwick family available to me.
[5] Coulson, p. 52-3.
[6] Interview with author, Johannesburg, 16 February 1999.
[7] KCM 3279a-d. Richmond School History, 3 October 1893 and Coulson, p. 286-88.
[8] The tray is in the possession of Mrs Clare Rossouw.

CHAPTER 3
Main sources consulted in this chapter

Atkins, Keletso E (1993) *The Moon is Dead! Give us our money! The Cultural Origins of an African Work Ethic, Natal, South Africa, 1843-1900.* Johannesburg: University of Witwatersrand Press.

Colony of Natal (1895) *Blue Book on Native Affairs.* Pietermaritzburg: Government Printers.

Guy, Jeff (1982) 'The destruction and reconstruction of Zulu society' in Marks, S and Rathbone, R, *Industrialisation and Social Change in South Africa: African Class Formation, Culture and Consciousness, 1870-1930.* London: Longman.

Harries, Patrick (1982) 'Kinship, ideology and the nature of pre-colonial labour migration: labour migration from the Delagoa Bay hinterland to South Africa up to 1895' in Marks, S and Rathbone, R, *Industrialisation and Social Change in South Africa: African Class Formation, Culture and Consciousness, 1870-1930.* London: Longman.

Harries, Patrick (1994) *Work, Culture and Identity: Migrant Labourers in Mozambique and South Africa c. 1860-1910.* Johannesburg: University of the Witwatersrand Press.

Katz, Elaine (1999) 'Revisiting the origins of the industrial colour bar in the Witwatersrand gold-mining industry 1891-1899,' *Journal of Southern African Studies.* 25:1 (March).

Lambert, John (1995) *Betrayed Trust: Africans and the State in Colonial Natal.* Durban: University of Natal Press.

Moodie, T Dunbar with Ndatshe V (1994) *Going for Gold: Men, Mines and Migration.* Johannesburg: University of the Witwatersrand Press.

Van Onselen, Charles (1982) *Studies in the Social and Economic History of the Witwatersrand 1886-1914. Vols I and II. New Babylon, New Nineveh,* Johannesburg: Ravan Press. Selected articles: '"*AmaWasha*": the Zulu washermen's guild of the Witwatersrand 1890-1914', 'Regiment of the Hills: "*Umkosi Wezintaba*": the Witwatersrand's lumpenproletariat army 1890-1920', '"The witches of suburbia": domestic service on the Witwatersrand 1890-1914'.

Notes
[1] Harries (1994), pp. 200-208, 280.
[2] Van Onselen, Vol. II, p. 33.
[3] Ibid, pp. 84, 79.
[4] Ibid, p. 175.
[5] Blue Book, p. 71.
[6] Ibid, p. 108.
[7] Guy, p. 186.
[8] Ibid, p. 187.

CHAPTER 4
Main sources consulted in this chapter

Colony of Natal (1897) *Blue Book on Native Affairs.* Johannesburg Office: Report by JS Marwick, pp. 23-31. Pietermaritzburg: Government Printers.

Katz, Elaine (1999) 'Revisiting the origins of the industrial colour bar in the Witwatersrand gold-mining industry 1891-1899,' *Journal of Southern African Studies.* 25:1 (March).

More information on Marwick's early career was found in KCM 2649, KCM 2596, Memorandum of Appointments held by JS Marwick previous to May 1900.

Newspaper reports discussed in this chapter were found in File 7, Killie Campbell Africana Library, Marwick Manuscript Collection (KCM). Some articles were not dated and a few have no reference to the newspaper in which the article appeared.

Notes
[1] KCM 2598b.
[2] Interview, 16 February 1999.
[3] News clippings, book 2.
[4] Ibid.
[5] *Blue Book* (1897), pp. 23-31. Most of the information in the following paragraphs was gleaned from this report.

[6] I am indebted to Elaine Katz for providing this information.

[7] KCM 2305, Diary of JS Marwick 1904.

[8] KCM 3672a-b, Letters to JS Marwick. Bongani Sithole translated these letters.

CHAPTER 5
Main sources consulted in this chapter

Marwick, JS (1900) Report relative to the exodus of Natal natives from the South African Republic, October 1899. Enclosure no. 77, *Blue Book: Further Correspondence Relating to Affairs in South Africa*. January. London: Printed for Her Majesty's Stationery Office. [Cd. 43] The report has been adapted from indirect speech to direct speech.

Marwick Manuscript Collection, File 7 'March with Zulus from Johannesburg to Natal, 9th to 16th October 1899'.

Telegrams to and from Marwick and his superiors in Natal are found in enclosure no. 61 from *Blue Book*. [Cd. 43] Joseph Chamberlain's comment on the report is found in enclosure no. 81.

Notes

[1] Marwick, pp. 167-72.

[2] *Standard and Diggers' News*, 4 October 1899.

[3] KCM 2571, Letter from Max, Marwick's nephew, 30 September 1934, accompanied by 'a quotation from Katie Makhanya's story ...'

[4] KCM 2607, Letter of L de Souza to JS Marwick, 4 October 1899.

[5] *Blue Book*, enclosure no. 61, pp. 130-32.

[6] KCM 2076b, Edith Clarke, 'Marwick's Memorable March', 'A' Programme 3/7/1945 8.45 p.m. (Edith Clarke was Marwick's eldest sister. In later years she told Marwick's grandchildren stories about the march, according to Marwick's granddaughter, Clare. Interview 16 February 1999.)

CHAPTER 6
Main sources consulted in this chapter

Breytenbach, JH (1949) *Die Tweede Vryheids-oorlog. Vol. II: 'Ontplooiing van die Boere offensief, Oktober 1899'*. Cape Town: Nasionale Pers.

Harrison, CW Francis (1903) *Natal: An Illustrated Official Railway Guide and Handbook of General Information*. London: Payne Jennings. All quota-

tions in this chapter are taken from pp. 129-146.

Mouton, JA (1957) 'Generaal Piet Joubert in die Transvaalse Geskiedenis' in *Archives Yearbook for South African History*. Pretoria: Government Printer.

Pakenham, Thomas (1979) *The Boer War*. Cape Town: Jonathan Ball.

Reitz, D (1929) *Commando: A Boer Journal of the Boer War*. London: Penguin. All quotations in this chapter are taken from pp. 23-31.

Marwick, JS (1900) Report relative to the exodus of Natal natives from the South African Republic, October 1899. Enclosure no. 77, *Blue Book: Further Correspondence Relating to Affairs in South Africa*. January. [Cd. 43] The main narrative of this chapter is based on this report. Note that indirect speech has been adapted to direct speech.

Notes

[1] Marwick, pp. 167-72.

[2] KCM 2571, 'A quotation from Katie Makanya's story'.

[3] In possession of Marwick's granddaughter, Clare.

[4] *Standard and Diggers' News*, 7 October 1899.

[5] Mouton, p. 233.

[6] Pakenham, pp. 104-105 and p. 603 footnote.

[7] My thanks to Robert Morrell for alerting me to this.

[8] Mouton, p. 234.

[9] Breytenbach, p. 107.

[10] *Standard and Diggers' News*, 1 November 1899.

CHAPTER 7
Main sources consulted in this chapter

The main source for this chapter is the interview with Marwick's granddaughter, Clare Rossouw (16 February 1999) as well as miscellaneous documents in the Marwick Manuscript Collection.

Notes

[1] KCM 2579, From Prime Minister to Marwick.

[2] KCM 2573a, Johannesburg representative, SNA Department, 20/10/1899.

[3] *Blue Book* [Cd. 43], enclosure 81 and KCM 2747.

[4] KCM 2544, Letter to JS Marwick from JFE Barnes, 14 Dec 1899.

[5] KCM 2598a, Letter to JS Marwick from W Hely-Hutchison.

[6] Transvaal Archives (TAB), MCP 120/121 42/01, SNA 35/1900. Memorandum from Intelligence Department, 3/9/1900.

[7] KCM 3196, News clippings book.

CHAPTER 8

Main sources consulted in this chapter

Amery, LS (1900) *The Times History of the War in South Africa*. Vol. I. London: Sampson Low, Marston & Co Ltd.

Breytenbach, JH (1949) *Die Tweede Vryheidsoorlog. Vol. II: 'Ontplooiing van die Boere offensief, Oktober 1899'*. Cape Town: Nasionale Pers.

Numerous newspaper clippings, some undated and some not stating the newspaper or magazine, were found in File 7 of the Marwick Manuscript Collection and in the news clippings books.

Stott, Clement C (1900) *The Boer Invasion of Natal*. London: SW Partridge.

Notes

[1] News clippings, book 2.

[2] KCM 2567, 'A Memorable March'.

[3] KCM 2942, Letter to JS Marwick from ND Hole, 1 Dec 1899.

[4] KCM 2746, *The Leisure Hour* of 1900.

[5] Stott, pp. 30-31. According to Clare Rossouw, Stott is related to the Marwicks via the Rowes.

[6] Marwick Manuscript Collection, File 7.

[7] KCM 2661, Letter to JS Marwick from J Mkwanazi.

[8] Pakenham, T (1979) *The Boer War*, p. 120.

PHOTOGRAPHIC ACKNOWLEDGEMENTS

I would like to acknowledge the following institutions who gave permission for the reproduction of photographic material in this book. My sincere appreciation, too, to the personnel for their assistance. Copyright to the photographic material rests with the various institutions.

• Department of Historical and Literary Papers and Map Collection, University of the Witwatersrand Library, Johannesburg: Michelle Pickover and Patrick Duncan.
• Johannesburg College of Education: Patricia Meyer.
• Killie Campbell Africana Library, Durban: Janet Twine and Lisa Stockman.
• MuseuMAfricA, Johannesburg: Kathy Brookes.
• Rare Book Collection, Rand Afrikaans University Library Services, Johannesburg: Henriette Latsky.
• Richmond, Byrne and District Museum: J Charmian Coulson and Gordon Manton.
• South African National Museum of Military History, Johannesburg: Gerda Viljoen and Susanne Blendulf.
• Transnet Heritage Foundation, Johannesburg: Eric Conradie and Tumi Mdlalo.

AUTHOR'S NOTE

It is customary for historians whose research results in a publication to acknowledge financial support. In this case thanks is due to Basil, Christiaan and Elsa who had to tolerate Marwick and the marchers not only as a continuous topic of conversation at the dinner table but as a temporary onslaught on the family budget.

Many other friends and colleagues joined the long march. Ena Jansen went along to Durban for the research where Christina Moller had done the prior reconnaissance and provided me with shelter. At the Killie Campbell Library, where copyright restrictions are imposed, Bongani Sithole copied and translated scores of Marwick documents at speed. Robert Morrell not only provided the link with David Hewson who told me about Marwick's grandchildren living in Johannesburg, but made valuable comments and generously shared research and information on the Old Natal Families.

Back in Johannesburg Carolyn Hamilton helped with leads to find information on pre-colonial Zululand, and Elaine Katz, the expert on gold mining on the Rand before the Anglo-Boer War, unstintingly delved through her archives to find answers to my questions.

My sister, Henriette Latsky, who heads the Rare Book Collection at the Rand Afrikaans University Library, answered queries at odd times and came up with interesting snippets. Thanks to Sifiso Ndlovu, Diana Vorster, Louise Jordaan and Jenny Birkett, who read the manuscript and made many good suggestions. Bonelela Memani checked the Zulu spelling.

A special word of thanks to Mrs Clare Rossouw, Marwick's granddaughter, who was willing to be interviewed and shared her memories of her grandfather. Finally, if editor Julie-Anne Justus had not commented that it was hard to picture the countryside which the marchers crossed, I would never had gone in search of more visual material. At the Transnet Heritage Library, Eric Conradie introduced me to their wonderful collection of 1890s NZASM photographs. It added a new dimension to the written record of the march. Publisher Annari van der Merwe's suggestion – to use direct speech instead of paraphrasing historical records – added another dimension. Hence an author's caution: The dialogue used in this book accurately reflects what was reported to have been said at the time and has in no way been fictionalised.